Overcoming

LIVING OUR
BEST LIFE
IN SPITE OF . . .

A COMPILATION BY PAT R. COLEMAN

Overcoming
Living Our Best Life In Spite Of...
Pat Coleman
BlessZing Publishing

Published by BlessZing Publishing, St. Louis, Missouri
Copyright ©2022 Pat Coleman
All rights reserved.

No part of this publication may be reproduced, stored in a retrieval system, or transmitted in any form or by any means, electronic, mechanical, photocopying, recording, scanning, or otherwise, except as permitted under Section 107 or 108 of the 1976 United States Copyright Act, without the prior written permission of the Publisher. Requests to the Publisher for permission should be addressed to Permissions Department, BlessZing Publishing – pat@patrcoleman.com

Limit of Liability/Disclaimer of Warranty: While the publisher and author have used their best efforts in preparing this book, they make no representations or warranties with respect to the accuracy or completeness of the contents of this book and specifically disclaim any implied warranties of merchantability or fitness for a particular purpose. No warranty may be created or extended by sales representatives or written sales materials. The advice and strategies contained herein may not be suitable for your situation. You should consult with a professional where appropriate. Neither the publisher nor author shall be liable for any loss of profit or any other commercial damages, including but not limited to special, incidental, consequential, or other damages.

All contributing authors to this analogy have submitted their chapters to an editing process and have accepted the recommendations of the editors at their own discretion. All authors have approved their chapters prior to publication.

Project Management and Book Design:
Davis Creative, LLC, CreativePublishingPartners.com

Editor: Marie Chewe-Elliott
Proofreader: Dr. Maurya Cockrell
Compilation by Pat R. Coleman

Publisher's Cataloging-In-Publication Data

Names: Coleman, Pat R., 1960- compiler.

Title: Overcoming : living our best life in spite of ... / [a compilation by Pat R. Coleman].

Description: St. Louis, Missouri : BlessZing Publishing, [2022]

Identifiers: ISBN 9798985718102 (paperback) | ISBN 9798985718119 (ebook)

Subjects: LCSH: Women, Black--Psychology--Anecdotes. | Women, Black--Social conditions--Anecdotes. | Women, Black--Crimes against--Anecdotes. | Resilience (Personality trait) in women--Anecdotes. | Self-actualization (Psychology) in women--Anecdotes. | Courage--Anecdotes. | LCGFT: Anecdotes.

Classification: LCC HQ1163 .O94 2022 (print) | LCC HQ1163 (ebook) | DDC 305.48896--dc23

ATTENTION CORPORATIONS, UNIVERSITIES, COLLEGES AND PROFESSIONAL ORGANIZATIONS: Quantity discounts are available on bulk purchases of this book for educational, gift purposes, or as premiums for increasing magazine subscriptions or renewals. Special books or book excerpts can also be created to fit specific needs. For information, please contact Pat Coleman – pat@patrcoleman.com, or visit patcolemanllc.com

DEDICATIONS

I dedicate this book in loving memory of my parents
Annie and Clarence Williams
and my sister Doris J. Harris.

And... I dedicate this book to my tribe...
my sister Alvera "Ree" Scott, and all the women in my life
who pray for me, who pray with me,
who encourage me, who believe in me,
and who bless me with their unwavering love.

I'M GRATEFUL

Thank you to each woman who contributed your voice
to this anthology. You all are beautiful, bold, boss ladies!
I am forever grateful for your brave heart and vulnerability
exhibited in this collection of overcoming stories.

-Pat Coleman

TABLE OF CONTENTS

Foreword by Brenda D. Newberry vii

Strong by Marie Chewe-Elliott. ix

Pat Coleman: Big Girl's Journey 1

Bryanna P. Williams: Growth through Grief 9

Ernestine Johnson: From Financial Freedom
          to Generational Wealth 17

Erica Williams: All Eyes on Me 25

Tiffany Lacy Clark: A.C.E.'d It: Overcoming
          Adverse Childhood Experiences 33

Dr. Alice Prince: Overcoming My Oh! Sh*t Moment. 41

Chaundra Tatum: Tragedy, Trauma, Triumph 49

Gisele Marcus: From Harlem to Harvard 57

Patricia Bosman: What's in a Name?. 65

Shaire Lynnette Duncan: It was Necessary 73

Marshá Reynolds: Overcoming My Perspective 81

Marion "Rossi" Kunney: My Stones are Now Diamonds 89

Charlotte Hammond: Strength to Overcome. 97

Sheena Williams: Changing the Narrative. 105

Alesha Henley: Banishing the Myth: "I'm not good enough" 111

Halima McWilliams: Living Up to My Name 117

Rachel R. Jackson: Go Through Your Valley 125

Lashanda Barnes: Overcoming Silence: Speaking My Power 133

Taraya J. Shirdan: Now…It's On Me 141

Alana Pease: Any Given Sunday 149

Rev. Angela M. Tate: Overcoming My 6 157

Devon Moody-Graham: Overcoming Yourself: Redefining You . . . 165

Leslie Doyle: Never Defeated 173

Vanessa Cooksey: The Three Ds of My PPP 181

Kynisha Ducre: Life in a Magical Box 189

Ronke Faleti: Future Pride: The Courage to Overcome 197

Sherry Sissac: Overcoming the Yes Syndrome 207

Simone M. Cummings: Your Path is What You Make It 215

Desiree Coleman-Fry: The Sound of Magic 223

Janelle Jenkins: Breaking the Mold 231

Kimberly Stemley: Are Giants Five Feet Tall? 237

Lisa Michelle Garnett: Don't Let Your Dreams
　　　　　　　　　　Turn Into Nightmares 245

Dr. Maurya D. Cockrell: Becoming the Grief Walker 253

Foreword

These things happen to me too! That is what those that are not Black often say or said when situations of bigotry, racism, inequality and inequity were shared...in the past. Often I would hear highly paid culture consultants say that what Black people share is mostly just anecdotal. The stories of hurt, challenge and dismay, occurring day-by-day. Anecdotal? Hardly. Same things happen to them? Not really. It is much different when these things happen due to something for which you are not responsible nor can you "pass," hide or ignore...the color of your skin. Even though the stories here may have elements of challenges around racism or bigotry, it is not the focus at all. As the name implies it is about overcoming within various areas of life, various careers and challenging as well as supporting families.

In this book 33 Black women share their stories, not as victims, but as Overcomers! All the challenges each of them have encountered, yet, they have arrived in a place of peace and comfort in their own skins. Not bitter. Wiser!

These stories are about human experiences within the very core of life itself. The challenges and disappointments but more importantly it is about their resolution to succeed in their own definition of success and also their path to achieve far beyond what was or is expected. These women are not sorrowful, angry, or resentful. It is a book about joy. The joy of a life that moves. A life that aspires and inspires. A life of achievement.

In these pages you will see and learn first hand what obstacles these writers had to overcome and see their strength, fortitude, and arrival at place that may have seemed impossible looking at their youth or backgrounds. Each story is unique yet heartwarming as you get taken in by their accounts. You not only read but also feel their pains, sorrows, and disappointments. You become proud of them as if they were within your own family. They worked, observed, challenged themselves and the system to get to their place of peace and their own success. These are not anecdotes but real life events. They include situations in which they had to tactfully intervene in order to ensure their children or spouses were safe in spite of the atrocities against them. Atrocities include gender barriers, neighborhood barriers, policy barriers and barriers within various systems.

This book is a must read for those that are challenged by adversity. Knowing that you are not alone in the challenging experiences. Knowing that your experience is not an anecdote but something that is real and has occurred to others. These women demonstrate that there are many ways to conquer adversity and they reveal that adversity is something that may occur many many many times over a lifetime. However, adversity is never a show-stopper. These women reveal that there are many ways to become an Overcomer.

Intelligent. Articulate. Strong. Gentle yet determined. Bold. Independent. Kind. Polite. Not victims at all. These women are Overcomers! Read about these special women and may you feel the power to become an Overcomer in your own right!

Brenda D. Newberry,
-Founder and Retired Chair & CEO, The Newberry Group, Inc.
-Independent Non-Executive Board Member, Spire Inc. (NYSE:SR)
-Author: *Navigating Your Landscape: Finding Your Path Using a Moral Compass*

Strong

I am black coffee,
tornadic winds,
rushing currents of the Mississippi
and the force behind Serena's serve.
I am the incredible, damn-near mythological
"here-I-come-to-save-the-day"
STRONG Black woman.
Carrying the weight of my family and the world,
Carrying babies without complaining
and without even appearing to strain.
Carrying dreams of the ancestors,
aspirations of the children and
standing as pillar of strength and
pillow of comfort for my husband.
Carrying trauma, carrying drama,
Strutting through life secretly
bleeding from compounded wounds of
micro and macroaggressions
bearing others' confessions
forgiving repeated transgressions
bandaging pain and sorrow
speaking hope for tomorrow
perfecting the mask
with style, grace and class
 because after all
 I am that

STRONG Black woman….
as if I've ever had a choice.

– Marie Chewe-Elliott

Pat Coleman

Big Girl's Journey

"My "Big Girl" grown self appreciates there is growth in overcoming what has and what will come my way during life's journey."

— Pat Coleman

Growing up in a family with five siblings (I was number four), I hadn't even begun to dream of what my own family would be like when the reality of it was staring me in the face or should I say belly. I was a student when I became a teenage mom of not one but two boys. As I was learning academics, I was also learning how to be a good mother.

Although my parents were not pleased with me becoming a mother at such a young age, they unconditionally loved the three of us. My nickname "Big Girl," coined by my Daddy, would present itself during tough, critical moments in my life. My big sis, Ree, said Daddy named me Big Girl because I was extremely smart and bossy as an infant and toddler.

I never imagined the many bumps in the road my boys and I would confront on our life's journey. It was not an easy one, not because of lack of money or support. My boys and I faced numerous other hurdles to overcome. The ugliest of them was discrimination. It came in intervals, and it would show its unbecoming face throughout my boys' schooling — with force and vengeful indignation. All along the way, "Big Girl" would rise to the occasion, and it was as if Daddy knew that nickname would be a source of strength for me when I needed it most.

I, Big Girl, raised two boys in this sometimes cruel world, especially to black boys and black men. Born 15 months apart, I can say without a doubt I never loved the way I loved my boys when they entered this world. They have taught me important life lessons and skills. I continue to be blessed by them every day.

My firstborn, an extrovert, acted as though he was born years before his brother. He consistently has taken on the true meaning of a big brother through his sage advice, spot-on know-how, and unyielding protection.

My baby, the introvert, is laid back. It takes quite a bit to get him riled. He's smart, and the quiet observer. He respects his brother and, likewise, will do anything for him. They have always had each other's back.

Both are successful grown men with wives and children, careers, and responsibilities. I take enormous pride in still talking about them in this way — my firstborn and my baby.

I want nothing but the best for my boys. When they were in first and third grade, I (Big Girl) transferred them from our urban school district environment to a well-funded, predominately white school district in the suburbs by participating in the desegregation program. They attended a blue-ribbon school, received an excellent education, and made lifetime friends. Little did I know, it would come with a price. They experienced unfortunate situations no child should ever experience.

As early as elementary school, my firstborn came home and told me a teacher would routinely bump up against him, sort of like pushing him out of the way. It took him a couple of times to share this before I fully understood. I called to meet with the teacher and school principal. The teacher, the principal, my pastor, and I gathered in a room. When I (Big Girl) shared my son's experience, the teacher stood and slammed her hand loudly on the table and fervently stated in a loud, stern voice that what I said was ridiculous and she didn't do such a thing.

As I looked at her, I clearly saw her anger and prejudice. Frankly, she was more upset I called her out than by the allegation itself. The principal immediately knew she was in the wrong, and to prove himself to be a caring individual, he picked up my boys and took them to lunch a couple of times. I knew the real reason he visited our home. As a young, black single mom with two sons, he wanted to see where and how I lived.

In those formative school years, before middle school, my baby said he had a teacher who would glaringly stare at him in a way that suggested, 'Why are you here?' Later in the year, that teacher was diagnosed with cancer. When my son told me about it, it saddened him. Even though he knew she didn't care for him, he felt compassion for her.

In high school, a teacher said to my son, "Why don't you stop acting like a crack baby!" That got to me, it really got to me. And to this day, it makes me angry to even think about it. I complained to the school, and sadly, nothing ever came of it.

My boys were athletes. One was a star football and basketball player and the other a star basketball player, both varsity starters on the basketball team. It was a joy to watch them excel in their games. I believe it was at that point they began to find their acceptance at school, because they helped the team win games.

While they were in high school, I met my husband, Harold. His supportive nature and presence went a long way as it does today.

Racial profiling for my boys began when they started to drive. The police harassed them more times than I could count. I'd often ask, "Why my boys?" I'd cry in private and talk to my dad, in heaven. I'd say, "Big Girl is having a rough time raising these boys!" He brought me comfort. I'd surrender my pain to God and then say to myself, "Big Girl is not having it!" I'd muster the strength to move on.

We made it through graduation with my firstborn, and I was overjoyed he was going away to college. Sadly, I soon discovered that another bump in the road would surface again. During his first semester, my son called to say he was kicked out of school for fighting.

For every minute of that four-hour torturous drive, I worried. I worried because I didn't know if my son was safe and who would protect him until we arrived. When we talked to the administration about what happened, they said he fought with a weapon. That weapon was his belt to fight and protect himself from two white boys (his roommate and his roommate's friend) who repeatedly mistreated him. The school would not work out a compromise, so we packed up his belongings and headed home.

Similarly, my baby boy had an unforgettable experience. He attended college approximately 45 minutes away from home, living on campus. One evening, when his brother, cousin and friends visited, they were kicked off campus AND my son was kicked out of school. He was told by school administration he invited "thugs" to the campus.

When my husband, son, and I went to the school to speak with the college president, he stood and aggressively pointed his finger directly at my face and with a most threatening tone said my son invited thugs to the campus. It was like a punch to my gut to have my son witness that ugly moment. "Big Girl" kept her composure (although my husband did not) and walked out of the room with my son.

It has always been my goal to do the best for my sons, to do everything in my power to help them succeed. It breaks my heart to know they both experienced such hardship simply because of the color of their skin.

The tipping point of my questioning "Why my boys?," "Why me?," "Why our family?" happened while my sons were helping my husband and me at our house with outdoor projects. One afternoon while they were working, the police arrived — with guns out. Someone reported my sons were breaking into a home.

Are you kidding me?

My sweet grandson was sitting at the kitchen table having a snack, and the police went as far as to go to the back door where my grandson could see. I pray my grandson, another black boy, does not have the same heart-wrenching experiences.

This uncalled occurrence grieved and outraged me. I became angry all over again, especially with the ongoing mistreatment of my sons. I became cynical and less trusting. Again, why us?

Through all the discriminatory experiences we've encountered as a family, I'm eternally grateful our not-so-smooth journey didn't derail my boys or me. Fortunately, the strong foundation my family was built upon along with my "Big Girl," traits navigated us through the rough patches, and we continue to and steadfastly move in the right direction.

In spite of the bumps in the road, I, Big Girl, managed to raise two wonderful young men and continue my education, earning an MBA. I've experienced entrepreneurship, I'm a CEO of a successful nonprofit, and I have a close relationship with God. What's more, I, Big Girl, have honored my father's legacy of resiliency, kindness, and perseverance, passing it along to his grandchildren and great-grandchildren.

Daddy would be proud.

Pat Coleman is president and CEO of Behavioral Health Response, Inc (BHR), a professionally staffed and accredited clinical contact center that provides expert behavioral health and crisis response services 24/7 to agencies and companies worldwide.

She is also the founder of Pat Coleman LLC, offering leadership coaching, speaking, and voice-over artistry. She is contributing author of Own Your Grit published in 2021.

Pat serves as a board trustee for Fontbonne University, board member of Greater St. Louis, Inc., and board director (Region 7) of the National Council for Mental Health Wellbeing.

She is a recipient of several awards, including the 2022 *St. Louis Titan 100*, *St. Louis Business Journal*, 2020 Most Influential Businesswoman, *St. Louis Business Journal*, 2018 Diverse Business Leader, *National Council for Mental Health Wellbeing*, 2016 Visionary Leader, and *The St. Louis American Foundation* Salute to Excellence in Healthcare 2012.

Pat integrates faith, family, and community by valuing innovation, remaining flexible to change, and committing to excellence through teamwork. She has a Master of Business Administration from Fontbonne University and a Bachelor of Science from Saint Louis University.

pat@patrcoleman.com
patcolemanllc.com/
www.linkedin.com/in/patriciarcoleman

Bryanna P. Williams

Growth through Grief

"The beauty in growing through what we go through is knowing that life moved on and took us with it."

Intro:

Although grief is often associated with a negative connotation, I like to think that my grief made a huge contribution to the young woman I am today.

People may say, "Why would you associate that with who you are? Don't you want to be all light and sunshine with no cloudy days?" I've dealt with depression and anxiety for many years, so some cloudy days come with the contract. I like to find the beauty and good in everything I experience. I try to find a lesson in every loss because anything can be a teachable moment. You may be familiar with the five stages of grief: *denial, anger, bargaining, depression, and acceptance*. But you may not know that we can grieve more than death. Over the years, I've grieved the loss of my loved ones, and I've also grieved past relationships, losing and outgrowing friendships, and the expectations I had set for myself and my mental health. I had this roadmap of what my life was supposed to be and who was supposed to be around for the long run.

As I matured and grew older, it was hard to move forward from that image I had set for myself. Not only do I want to talk about my experience with grief, but how to support someone who is grieving. For this chapter, I will share the general order of the stages of grief, but it is also important to remember that grief has no linear timeline. We can experience the phases of grief at different moments and times in our life. We also cannot put a time limit on how long we grieve. Grief is unique to each person who experiences it; no one person's journey will look like the next.

Phase I: Denial

I was grieving and didn't even realize it. Some call it denial. I remember being a senior in high school and my mom telling me that my grandmother, Marion, was no longer in remission. Looking back, I remember feeling like my senior year was the worst year of my life. I was losing friends, having conflicts with others that I didn't understand, and my then-boyfriend had gone away to college. I felt alone and misunderstood, so I couldn't fathom losing someone else in my corner. My spunky, spirited grandmother had just been in her treasured garden asking me to hand her the garden shears and to help her pull weeds. She chased me around her house with a wet rag laughing and singing "Bossy" by Kelis and "Air Force Ones" by Nelly. My granny, my Franny, couldn't possibly be sick. No, my granny did not deserve this; someone less passionate and caring did. According to the Kübler-Ross Grief Cycle, denial can include avoidance, confusion, joy, shock, and fear. I found myself wanting to talk less and observe more. I thought no one could possibly understand how I was feeling, so why should I even try explaining myself?

Phase II: Anger

Unexpectedly, I lost my great grandfather, my Pops, while still grieving my grandmother's cancer. Then, I honestly lost a part of myself and replaced it with anger.

That pain a change you and them ill feelings a never compare to
that hole you got
See, now I know how that grief you got can really turn into hate
How you push everybody away, they all ungrateful anyway
How you never knew this amount of love would cause so much pain
that you rather hate take its place
Rather never love at all than to let it all fall away
It's in one fall that you resolve it all
Don't need nobody cause at the end of the day,
I'm the one I gotta face
I see the regret all in ya face
How you wish you could take the place
Can look nobody in the eyes because all
you see is an enemy in the place
If you can't take my pain away, why you even in my space?
Wasn't there for me then, my misery don't love company,
so please don't try to comfort me now
All my loved ones gone, I just wanna be alone
in my own solitude
I don't care how you take it
This pain right here, it can't be mistaken

Phase III: Bargaining

In the following two years, I had lost my grandmother, three uncles, my aunt, and my great-grandmother. I felt like everyone I loved was leaving me and blamed myself for growing up and "neglecting" them. I felt total despair. I started questioning everything, even myself. How could I dare be out enjoying life with my friends when I should have been spending time with my family? Why had I wasted so much time surrounded by people who didn't even appreciate my family or me? Inside that guilt was still anger, making me doubt myself and my relationships with others. Back then, I felt that if I couldn't go back in time to change everything, I deserved to suffer and wallow in my misery.

Phase IV: Depression

The scary thing about depression is that sometimes you don't remember most of it. You sink so low, and it gets so dark. It's like the sunken place how you're trapped in your body mindlessly living day by day. You sleep more, care less, indulge more, end up less patient and more irritable.

And if you haven't figured it out, I mean me. I did all of those things and then some, but do I remember? Nope. I have very little memory of my darkest days. What I do remember is longing. Longing for my family back. Longing for my friends that I separated from. Longing for my almost five-year relationship that had ended. Longing for the life I had planned as the ambitious little girl I used to be. Longing to know what my purpose here even was. I felt so lost and disconnected from everything.

Phase V: Acceptance

Nora McInerny once said, "Everyone you know has a 100% chance of dying." She couldn't have said it better. I learned to accept the cycles of life and appreciate everyone and everything in the moment. I also learned that just because a friendship or relationship has ended doesn't mean you can't still appreciate the times you shared. Every person in your life teaches you something. Each adds to all of the little pieces that make you, you. Here are some things I learned that I feel will be helpful to you and others grieving:

- Guilt is normal and can show up in different ways.
- Acceptance is not the finish line. There might be days when you relapse, but one thing for sure is that you'll continue growing.
- When supporting someone who is grieving, they don't want you to tell them how they should feel or how long to grieve. Just let them know that you are present and supportive.
- We shouldn't just move on and pack every little thing we feel up for later. Saying "just stay strong" isn't acceptance. We should acknowledge and process our emotions so that we may move FORWARD.

It's true when they say that one chapter ends so the next can begin. My grief increased my levels of empathy, understanding, patience, and forgiveness for others and myself.

Despite my grief, I continue to grow in ways I couldn't have imagined. I developed healthy coping mechanisms for those days when I'm feeling low, and life seems to be too much.

I gained new flourishing friendships with women who motivate and inspire me daily. After not finishing my college education, I didn't know what I would make of myself.

At age 25, I work full-time as a program coordinator during the week, providing service for young adults in the city of St. Louis. I help them gain skills needed to follow their career paths and build employer connections.

During the weekends, I focus on perfecting my craft, braiding hair. I started my own business, Vyrgo by Bry, to invest in myself and the future I want.

I no longer need to find purpose around me because I gave myself purpose. I won't say I have everything figured out, but I will say that I continue to give my all and put my best foot forward.

I am overcoming, in spite of…

Bryanna P. Williams is a friend, a daughter, a sister, a mentor, and an entrepreneur. She is the founder of Vyrgo by Bry where she provides hair braiding services to those across the St. Louis area. She is also manifesting the expansion of her company to one day become a full-service beauty bar.

Bryanna also serves as the program coordinator of STL Youth Jobs at SLATE/EDSI Solutions. She works with the St. Louis Public High School seniors to connect them with employment in their desired career paths. During the summer, she serves St. Louis City youth, ages 16-24, with job readiness and financial literacy training, and helps them gain early work experience and exposure to different career paths. Bryanna herself was a former participant in STL Youth Jobs and was later hired as a full-time employee. She loves supporting the program that started her career.

Bryanna is passionate about providing her generation with positivity and encouragement. She is blessed with an amazing support system and strives to build that for others. In her spare time, she enjoys reading, taking long walks, shopping, and spending time with her family.

www.instagram.com/vyrgobybry?utm_medium=copy_link
www.linkedin.com/in/bryanna-williams-729a64157

Ernestine Johnson

From Financial Freedom to Generational Wealth

"Only when the pain of the same is greater than the pain of change will we begin to change."
— Larry Burkett, Crown Financial Ministries

I felt like I was on top of the world as I walked around with my 10 – 12 credit cards in my wallet, $30,000-plus student loan, and a $25,000 car loan. I had every credit card you can imagine! Oh, don't judge me! I paid the minimum amount due on each bill on time every month! I had no idea that a trap had been set for me and countless others.

You see, the Bible says in Proverbs 22:7 NKJV: "The rich rule over the poor and the borrower is slave to the lender!" I felt enslaved because I owed the credit card companies, who loved me because they knew that I and many other credit cardholders would only pay the minimum balance due each month. This meant that we would be accruing loads of interest each month. I continued on this path for many years, not realizing that I was in debtor's prison.

Throughout the years, I would listen to various experts on getting out of debt, and I would purchase a book here or a course there to help me get out of debt. Still, within a few months, I would lose interest in the information and continue back in my secure bondage routine. Several more years would pass, and I was perfectly fine spending up to my limits and making the minimum payments on all of my cards. On a Sunday afternoon during church service, where the topic was getting out of debt, my pastor mentioned a financial guru named Dave Ramsey and how his teachings were helping many families and individuals become debt-free. Once again, my curiosity was peaked. The next day I just happened to be in one of the Christian bookstores, and there was a book titled "The Total Money Make Over" by Dave Ramsey. I thought to myself, "This must be a sign!" I immediately purchased the book! I got home and started reading it and could not put it down. I was blown away by the stories of individuals and families in much deeper debt than me and how they became debt-free by following a few simple steps. After reading a few chapters, I decided that ENOUGH WAS ENOUGH, AND I WANTED TO BE DEBT FREE and ultimately be financially free!

As stated in the book, I began to gather my debts and get them in order from smallest to largest. I finished the book in a couple of days. I then decided that I would like to go on this debt-free journey. I found Dave Ramsey's 13-week Financial Peace University (FPU) class was scheduled in the St. Louis area, and I registered for the course. It was very refreshing to hear everyone's story and their progress on the road to becoming debt-free!! I was happy to share my journey with the group each week. I suggested to my pastor that we rethink starting an FPU class at our church since we could never get it off the ground in the past. (You know, if you make a suggestion in church, you're heading up the initiative). He was excited about the idea, and we began promoting FPU in our church. I taught the class with my husband and another couple, and we helped many people start their journey to becoming debt-free. We helped hundreds to implement the 7 Baby Steps as outlined in the Financial Peace course:

1. Save $1000 in a beginner emergency fund.
2. Pay off all debt (except the house) using the debt snowball method.
3. Put 3 – 6 months of expenses in savings for a full emergency fund.
4. Invest 15% of your household income into Roth IRAs and pre-tax retirement plans.
5. Save for your children's college education using tax-favored plans.
6. Pay off the house early.
7. Build wealth and give.

I continued reading and listening to anything I could get my hands on that talked about being debt-free and financial freedom! We were making a difference in our church, but that wasn't enough for me. I wanted to impact more individuals throughout the St. Louis Region. Approximately 30 months into my debt-free journey, I was able to scream those three magical words, "I'm DEBT-FREE!"

I can still remember the day I received that beautiful letter in the mail from the infamous "Sallie Mae" stating that I had completely paid off my student loan! I was finally there, and I continued to help others get there. I decided to become a Certified Financial Counselor and start my own business, Xkwsit (pronounced Exquisite) Money Matters, LLC. I traveled to Tennessee to attend Dave Ramsey's Counselor Training. My eyes were opened even more after the counselor training. I started researching financial gurus of color and reading and listening to what they had to say about financial fitness. I listened to Lynn Richardson's Millionaire Roundtable, and I read and participated in Michelle Singletary's book challenge, "The 21 Day Financial Fast". These two powerhouses were making huge positive impacts within African American communities across the country. I began speaking at churches and women's groups in the St. Louis area about getting out of debt and becoming financially free. I was making an impact, but it wasn't enough!

This information expanded my mind, and once your mind expands, it can never go back to the way it was. I started doing more research on wealth in the African American community, and I was very disappointed in what I was finding. The Black-white wealth gap is not an accident but rather the result of centuries of federal and state policies that have systematically facilitated the deprivation of Black Americans, says the Center for American Progress: "From the brutal exploitation of Africans during slavery to systematic oppression in the Jim Crow South to today's institutionalized racism — apparent in disparate access to and outcomes in education, health care, jobs, housing, and criminal justice — government policy has created or maintained hurdles for African Americans who attempt to build, maintain, and pass on wealth," the researchers wrote. This information may be shocking to some, but not most of us. I began wondering what I could do to help close this staggering racial wealth gap. I thought, "Am I my brother's keeper?" I would say for me, yes!

We must continue to invest in ourselves, our families, and our communities as well. Legacy is the new currency! The only way we begin to close the wealth gap and leave a legacy for our families is to think outside of the box. Heck, we need to get rid of the box and do things that we've never done before. To put us on a level playing field and help close the wealth gap, we need to diversify our financial portfolio by investing in the digital ecosystem. You will have to be living under a rock if you have not heard of cryptocurrency, specifically Bitcoin or the foreign exchange (Forex) Market. If you've ever traveled abroad and exchanged your countries' currency for another countries currency, you've participated in the Forex Market. I was introduced to the digital currency industry about three years ago. I read and learned about investing in bitcoin and trading in the Forex and CryptoCurrency space within the last year.

I have begun to diversify my financial portfolio. I am also helping family and friends do the same by investing in the digital currency space and building generational wealth to help bridge the wealth gap. By doing this, we can truly begin to leave a legacy for our children's children!

Ernestine Johnson is CEO of Xkwsit (pronounced Exquisite) Money Matters, LLC, a Financial Consulting Company. Prior to retiring in December 2013, she was employed by the United States Department of Agriculture as a Realty Specialist for over 36 years.

Ernestine started her Journey to Financial Freedom in 2008 when she enrolled in Dave Ramsey's 13-week Financial Peace University (FPU) Class that would transform her life forever. Upon completion, she led a six-week Crown Financial Ministries Road to Financial Freedom class and a four-week Crown Financial Ministries Money Matters class. She hosted and coordinated fifteen Dave Ramsey 13-week Financial Peace University classes, helping hundreds of families paying off over $200,000 in debt. Ernestine continues to conduct financial workshops and seminars throughout the St. Louis Area.

She aspires to help bridge the wealth gap within her community and culture by learning about the Foreign Exchange (Forex) and Cryptocurrency markets. Ernestine feels that by sharing her personal story of becoming debt-free, others will see that they, too, can live in financial peace, build wealth, and leave a legacy for their families.

Xkwsit0822@gmail.com

www.instagram.com/xkwsit

Erica Williams

All Eyes on Me

Overcome is a verb. The definition is: Succeed in dealing with a problem or difficulty.
Example: She worked hard to overcome.

    As I write my contribution to the **Overcoming** anthology book, I look at my surroundings. I'm in the beautiful five-bedroom home that I share with my fine husband and five-year-old son. My legs are crossed in Lotus pose with my computer perched on my lap. I look around the modernly designed room that includes a contemporary green couch with two accent chairs, brown and off-white luxury fabric with stainless steel legs stylish with elegant finishes. To my right is the most beautiful backyard you could imagine. The feeling of peace and tranquility overwhelms me. I know that I am blessed and have come a long way. I have worked very hard and deserve everything that this world's creator has in store for me. I pour myself a glass of wine and ask myself, "How did you get here?"

    I allowed myself to be quiet and think about my journey for the first time. I am living the American dream of marriage, motherhood, and entrepreneurship. So, this is not a sad story at all. It is my truth. I close my eyes and vividly remember my very first encounter with overcoming.

It was March 31, 1996, and I was just a young girl. I awoke to the most horrific scream you could imagine. I still hear it to this day. It was my mother. My 21-year-old brother was killed by gun violence. That was a great tragedy, and I grieved the loss of my brother tremendously. I had no clue how that would change our family's life trajectory. Before his death, I was the most sheltered little girl you can imagine. I was not even allowed to go in certain sections of my grandmother's home, like the basement or off the porch, which was a 4 x 4 space at best.

After his death, I began walking to the local store and meeting friends and foes two and three blocks away. It's not because I was allowed to do so, but because everyone around me was grieving, and no one noticed. "All eyes on me," by Tupac Shakur, was a double disk CD. It was the last piece of music purchased by my brother, Larry Antione Pearson Sr. Ironically, Tupac was also killed by gun violence in September of that year. I listened to that CD night and day. It became a soundtrack for that moment in time. For me, that was the best and worst thing that could have happened. I went pretty much where I wanted, whenever I wanted. Each time I would go further and further, learning and exploring the world through a different set of eyes and without guardianship. It was nothing but God's grace and mercy that saw me through.

My family eventually healed as best it could from a situation like that. But by the time they were paying attention to me again, I had gotten a taste of freedom, and I would never let it go. At 17, I decided to move out on my own. At the time, I don't know if they believed I had what it took to be on my own on my journey to adulthood. But all the morals and values they instilled still hold with me today. Adulting was the most empowering thing I had ever experienced. I was willing to take whatever came with that. Moving out meant leaving the security and comforts my family had provided for me to live in a small apartment with nothing. My grandmother made one visit and took me to the furniture store.

I believe most would describe me as a hard worker, and I got that mostly from my grandmother, Charline Pearson. I watched her work two jobs, go to church two or three times per week for choir rehearsal, and make Sunday dinner with me alongside her every weekend. I'll never forget when we went to the car dealership so that she could purchase a brand-new Lincoln Town Car right off the showroom floor. "Erica," she said with a southern accent, "Which car should I get?" I picked the tannish brown one, and she turned to the dealer and said, "That's the one. You heard her."

My mother was the same way. There was never anything too good if you wanted it. If you want something, you work for it, and it will come to you. When I think about my mother, class and sophistication immediately pop into my head. The woman tilts the room for sure. I come from a long line of successful women in their own right — from my grandmother to my mother and aunts.

My grandmother was also a praying woman, and we'd pray before everything. Gospel music was a staple. If she wasn't listening to it, she was singing it. She also never let anyone mistreat me, and she always told me to do the same. "Never let nobody mistreat you," she said. Once my uncle teased me as I was on my way to bed. I was wearing a scarf on my head to secure my hairstyle for the next day. My uncle said, "Binky," (my nickname he called me) "You look like Aunt Jemima." He laughed, but oh,

I cried and ran to my grandmother's arms. "What happened?" she asked. "He called me a bad name," I said. She went right into the living room and said to him, "What did you call her? Don't you ever say that to her again!" Then she turned to me and said, "Don't pay him no mind. You're beautiful, and you have to keep your hair together for church." She grabbed my hand and took me into her bedroom to go to bed. This is a funny story now, but I learned that you never let anyone define you. You define you.

My Aunt Linda was a true fashionista. She always had the most fly clothes, car, and house to match. She was always working hard. I love me some Aunt Linda, and I still channel her fashion sense to this day. I can rock an outfit and look in the mirror, and I'll say, "Now that's a Linda Reed outfit right there!" LOL! My Aunt Ann is smart as a whip. I mention these women because they were the first to shape me into the woman I am today. I want to give the reader a glimpse of why I may move the way I move, say the things I say, or wear the clothes I wear.

Being influenced by these women taught me to stay connected to whoever brings out the best in you. I've pretty much always done the right thing when it counts. I have always been thankful for where my life is at the moment. If this is all God had in store for me, I am all right with that. God has repeatedly shown me that he has more in store for me and stop playing myself small. This message is one I now preach to others.

Have you ever gone through a situation and looked back when you came out on the other side and thought, "WOW, that was crazy!" Or realized that what was meant to break you, was a test, and you passed with flying colors? Sometimes we see a picture or hear a song like the Tupac CD, and it reminds us of what you pushed past and prevailed on. I know that overcoming takes consistency, and without that, you kill your chance for success. Having your mental in check is a must. One positive thought can change your whole day. You can drink all the water, work out, and take vitamins, but if you don't take care of the problem in your head, you won't be healthy enough to prevail.

I'd be lying if I said my success was all about me. The love of my life is my husband, Cortez Williams. With him, I've been blessed with a rare love that I'm finding out more and more isn't so common. This man has pushed me to limits that I never imagined, and his confidence has most certainly rubbed off on me. He saw things in me that I didn't even see in myself - such as entrepreneurship. After obtaining my Associate's degree in medical billing and coding, I just wanted to work from home, billing for a doctor or insurance company. However, Cortez, my boyfriend at the time, knew I was destined for so much more. He invested his money into starting a home health care agency and located small office space, computers, etc. He said, "Quit your job. You can't do this part-time." Was I scared? Of course, I was. Who doesn't like guaranteed money from a secure job? But I also knew that when they made one job, they didn't stop, and I could always find a new job. So, I quit my 9 to 5 and became the business owner of Corica Group Home Health Care. I asked God to teach me to speak the right words at the right time and guide me on my journey, and He did just that.

So, for me, overcoming is about putting God first, staying grounded, working hard, and keeping people around you who love you and want to see you win. You shouldn't go where you aren't celebrated, where you don't feel loved, or someone is hating on you. When you surround yourself with negativity, you're self-sabotaging. Everything you pray for or post on social media can be yours. You have to stop making excuses and looking for a way out. Everything you need is already within you. My soundtrack for this moment is a song called "Grinding all my life" on the "Victory Lap" album by Nipsey Hussle.

And just like that, I open my eyes and see my beautiful home with the love of my life and my son and bonus daughter. I am overcoming.

Erica Williams currently owns and operates a business in a disadvantaged community. She is president and CEO of Corica Group Home Health Care, a Home Health Service agency based in St. Louis, Missouri. The agency is a trusted home health care that has provided services since 2013 and is a trusted and valued resource in the community. She is also the founder of Corica Group Adult Daycare, a facility that is an ideal alternative for seniors and people with disabilities.

She is a licensed pharmacy technician and has earned certifications in both medical billing and coding. She has more than 14 years of experience in health care. Erica also has more than 10 years of entrepreneurial and project management experience and has leveraged resources, including fiscal and budget management.

She is married to Cortez Williams and has two children, Bryanna Williams and Cortez Williams Jr. She is a woman of faith and loves empowering anyone she meets. Her mission is to empower people with disabilities to increase their independence through choice and opportunity.

Erica is currently creating Corica Group health compound, which would be office space, adult daycare, residential care facility, skilled nursing, and on-site physical therapy.

linkedin.com/in/erica-williams-56366b229

www.coricagroup.com

Tiffany Lacy Clark

A.C.E.'d It: Overcoming Adverse Childhood Experiences

I am overwhelmed with this sense of fear and panic. My eyes are open, but it's like what I'm seeing is distorted. It's like I am watching a movie starring myself. I am watching myself. The room seems large and cold. I can sense multiple people in the room. My consciousness is hovering above me as my physical body is on a couch in a dark basement. Paul is sexually assaulting my two-year-old body.

This, unfortunately, is the first memory of my life. And it is burned into my brain like a cattle brand. The unshakeable fear and paralysis that I felt in that moment are forever burned into my psyche. There would be three more men in the first six years of my life that did unspeakable things to my body, mind, and spirit.

I was awakened from my youthful slumber and assaulted more times than I care to remember. I still struggle to sleep at night because of my experiences with the real monsters that appeared on the cover of night. The boogeyman was not a fictional character for me. He was a family friend or beloved relative. He was very real and did not live in my mind or lurk under my bed. He sat at the kitchen table, and he shared laughs with my family that had no idea about any of the horrors that were happening.

Abuse, neglect, poverty, and all the perils that come with it have been very real and present parts of my life. As the oldest child of a young teen parent with a history of trauma, abuse, and neglect herself, there was little guidance in our early years. That dynamic of generational trauma and unhealed wounds led to many turbulent moments in my young life. Many of the dips and bumps in life felt like sure signs of the end. Yet there were some 'flight attendants' that popped up along the journey that thankfully helped me get back on course.

One of these attendants righted my flight path and helped me learn the value of increasing the altitude of my life, dreaming, and working hard to be whomever I wished despite my past traumas. George was a man that stumbled upon my mother, brother, and me during an outing in downtown East St. Louis. The memory of meeting him is also burned into my brain. He took us to eat, and I remember my 3- or 4-year-old eyes glaring at him with distrust the entire meal. Given my limited understanding of the world at that time and my sexual abuse, I was flooded with fear and anger whenever new men were introduced into my life. We went home with him after dinner.

This trip to his house ended our time living in an abandoned house. Though the house was abandoned, there was a discarded space heater and old canned foods that we warmed up by sitting them in front of the heater. That heater served as a stove, light, and protection from the frigid cold. Despite the environment and lack of resources, I felt safe there. We were alone, and there were no men there. It was just my mother, brother, and I sitting in front of that heater, eating Vienna sausages and mixed vegetables for breakfast, lunch, and dinner. I remember that time as an enjoyable time and not as a poor kid eating barely anything with no end in sight.

We never saw that house again after we moved into George's home. He changed everything. He had a very modest home, but he shared it with us and made it a safe place to the best of his ability. He made us feel welcomed. Eventually, that became home, and he became daddy. Being much older than my mom and from a vastly different kind of family, he stepped into the daddy role with ease. His presence and priorities were different. He showered my brother and me with love and attention. He loved us like we were always meant to be his kids. He spent every free moment he had, taking us to museums and parks and exploring every pond, duck, and pretend rocket ship in St. Louis.

Those times were so constant and his love so soft and safe that he gained my trust. I eventually confided in him about the sexual abuse that I was experiencing when he was away. My older cousin had come to stay with us for an extended period, and during that time, he began to violate my 4/5/6-year-old body in ways that I cannot bring myself to describe. This went on repeatedly, and he would sneak into the room shared by my brother and me and convince us to play "hide and seek." He never looked for my brother, but he always found me. I remember these times but in a very dissociated and movie-like way. It is like a bad movie starring me and being watched by me against my will; or a bad dream that went on and on with no way to wake myself. It is hard to describe how my mind created distance between itself and my physical body. The will to survive and be safe can manifest itself in many ways. Dissociation was my way to protect myself.

But there was a man I trusted and told about the game my cousin was making us play. What happened next was a blur. I remember my daddy crying and shaking. Suddenly, my daddy held my cousin against a wall with his feet lifted entirely off the ground. My cousin looked terrified. I had not known my daddy to be anything but kind and gentle, so I did not know how to process what was happening. A mix of fear, sadness, hopelessness, and anger washed over me, and I cried. I cried because I loved my daddy. I cried because I made him sad and then mad. I cried because I still loved my cousin despite what he had done to me. I cried because my mom was crying and begging my daddy to let my cousin go. I cried because my daddy let my cousin go with tears falling and arms shaking. As he dropped my cousin to the ground, he let out this belly aching wail and punched the glass door next to him. He ended up cutting his arm, and there was blood everywhere. I felt like in the end, the only people hurt were daddy and me.

Soon after that incident, we left the security of my daddy's house. My mother, brother and I got a new place to stay. My cousin came with us. But there were no more nights of any men slipping into my bed while I slept or any more "hide and seek" games played. That 6-year cycle had finally ended. I felt like the cost of ending that cycle was so painful that I battled with if I did the right thing by telling and disrupting the good that was present just because 'bad' things were happening to me.

That moment changed me. I started mourning the girl I was supposed to be and who was taken away from me before I ever had the opportunity to know her. I would live in that state of quietly mourning myself for 33 more years. At 38 years old, I finally decided that I needed to love myself more. I got a therapist, spiritual routine, and personal trainer. I sat with my anger, sat with grief, and started doing the real work of overcoming. I decided to protect myself from anyone that was causing harm to me emotionally, mentally, or physically — that included protecting me from the old me. I had to sit and process some ugly truths about my childhood and how it impacted my adult life.

I have experienced every adverse childhood experience on the assessment. The prizes for this perfect storm of trauma were horrible physical and mental health outcomes. Adverse childhood experiences can lead to post-traumatic stress disorder, anxiety, depression, suicidal thoughts, and suicide attempts. An adult living with their A.C.E.s can experience chronic over or under-eating, alcohol dependence, domestic violence, high blood pressure, stroke, attachment issues, and physical manifestations of high-level stress in the body.

Life has been turbulent, but I decided to stay the course on my journey to healing, dealing, and overcoming. I leaned into the mantra that my attitude would determine my altitude. I decided to get up above the storms and fly high. Using therapy, prayer, meditation, grace, tenacity, patience, fortitude, resilience, self-reflection, and the love from my daddy, I am on an upward climb. And it's only up from here! I haven't overcome, but I am overcoming!

Tiffany Lacy Clark, chief operating officer at Behavioral Health Response, Inc. (BHR), is responsible for the organization's day-to-day operations. She moves projects from concept to implementation and develops strategies that align with BHR's short- and long-term goals. With over 17 years of experience in behavioral health and business administration, she is also a licensed child welfare specialist and a certified qualified human services professional.

Tiffany worked for the Illinois Department of Human Services in the Division of Developmental Disabilities. She also served as executive director of Region 5 Metro East of the Illinois Division of Mental Health. Before coming to BHR, Tiffany worked at Places for People as vice president of clinical operations providing oversight for all clinical activities.

As an advocate for social justice and community development, Tiffany exhibited impressive leadership skills as a youth. Raised in Cahokia, IL, she spent a great deal of time creating and participating in volunteer groups and programs to uplift the community.

Community outreach and engagement is Tiffany's passion. She works within the East St. Louis community and currently works to facilitate a regional approach to jail diversion and treatment access for those with behavioral health conditions.

As a first-generation college graduate, Tiffany's family instilled the importance of education as the path to equity and resource attainment. She will complete her doctoral degree in business psychology/organizational leadership at The Chicago School of Professional Psychology and receive her Ph.D. in 2022.

www.linkedin.com/in/tiffany-lacy-Clark-51ba839b
www.facebook.com/tiffany.lacyclark.9
Tlacyclark@yahoo.com

Dr. Alice Prince

Overcoming My Oh! Sh*t Moment.

Regaining your purpose and power is hard as a professional black woman. Regaining your purpose and power is especially hard after having an "Oh! Shit" moment in your career. An "Oh! Shit," moment is what I would define as an experience that is unexpected, embarrassing, polarizing, and public. I had an "Oh! Shit" moment, which changed my life.

I worked for an institution for over ten years. I thought I would retire from the institution. I loved what I did, and I loved helping the community. I was in education and workforce. My job required a different skill set every day, and I loved it. Some days, I wrote contracts; some days, I wrote curriculum and workshops. Other days I helped young people get jobs or showed them how to open checking accounts. I would travel to learn what is happening in the education and workforce industries around the country. I served on multiple boards and was frequently asked to give keynote speeches.

I started my career as a Youth Manager, was elevated to a Director, and elevated to Executive Director. The Executive Director was the top position. I never thought in a million years that I would receive the top position in the agency. I am not sure why I never thought I was smart enough or strong enough to lead a twenty-five-million-dollar agency, but I did not think of myself in that capacity. I had my head down doing the work. I had been working at the agency for over ten years. I received numerous honors from many people and organizations, including Governor Jay Nixon, the Urban League, Better Family Life, 100 Black Men, and many more. I had been recognized as a technical assistance specialist by the Department of Labor and other agencies that supported youth and workforce programs.

Additionally, I loved the workforce because I understood the importance of providing good wages to our community. I also understood that one of the root causes of crime in my city was poverty. One way to mitigate poverty is helping the community obtain good jobs with good wages. Finally, to ensure I met the community's needs, I earned a doctorate degree in education. Education is a critical element of workforce development. I had done all the things that would prepare me for the role of Executive Director.

What I thought was the best professional move of my life by accepting the position as the Executive Director soon became the deadliest move of my life. The position killed my spirit. The position destroyed my reputation. I felt as if someone I loved and trusted stabbed me in the back with a double edge sword. The drama and trauma had me buried alive and left me for dead. It was the hardest moment of my professional life. I had experienced an "Oh, Shit" moment.

Oh! Shit.

Soon after I became the Executive Director, a calculated revolt had begun. Some people intentionally planned the revolt to oust me, embarrass me, persecute me, and ruin my professional career. The plan was awful, sad, and horrendous. Being the Executive Director was a hard and painful journey. It was a journey I had to endure.

I regained my power and purpose. My test is now my testimony. I knew that if God brought me to it, HE would bring me through it.

How Did I Make it through?

I am a faithful woman. I believe if God brings you to it, He will bring you through it. My faith went into overdrive. I knew that my test would one day be my testimony. I knew that I would regain my strength learning from my struggle one day. I would find power in my pain. I understood that there would be a powerful message from the painful mess I found myself in at the time. God makes what seems impossible, possible. I was obedient and faithful.

Isaiah 54

Deuteronomy 28

Psalms 18

Psalms 20

Romans 8

Harnessed Power

I harnessed my power and took inventory. I took inventory of my knowledge, education, and skill set. I took inventory of the things I cared most about and the things I enjoyed doing. I listed industries I wanted to learn more about. I listed some demands that would be non-negotiable in my next career. I harnessed my power by controlling my life, future, and destiny. I used my inventory list and began to map out my next professional journey.

I performed a SWOT analysis on myself. I wanted to be clear and reconcile my strengths, weaknesses, opportunities, and threats. It was important for me to grow from the whole experience, not just the painful part. As women, we often put the pain we have experienced at the center of our life, and we should not. The pain is part of the journey, but it is not the whole journey. The painful experience from the previous employer was below 10% of the time I was there. Meaning the other 90% was great. I used the entire experience to create a holistic SWOT analysis. I knew that I needed to control my professional journey. I wanted to be a better version of myself for myself. I needed to control my narrative and outcome.

The next phase of harnessing my power came from God. I knew I needed to get closer to God and build a different relationship with him, not because I was hurting but because I wanted to be healed by the Holy Spirit. I have always been a faithful servant. I prayed and spoke to God daily. I believed I had an amazing relationship with Him, but I knew I needed more this time. I needed the relationship to be more intimate. I needed to get in a desert-like atmosphere and pray. I went into isolation. I went into isolation because I wanted to only hear from God. I did not want a distortion of God's message. I wanted to understand my next assignment. It was clear that my next assignment was ME!

God said no weapon formed against you shall prosper. He did not say they would not form. I knew because I had survived, my life had a greater purpose. I knew it was time for me to find purpose in my pain, and God would be my catalyst for prosperity in my life. I began to affirm the prosperity God had placed on my life. Death and life live in the power of the tongue. I began to speak health, healing, and prosperity over my life and my family's life. I began to say things like I am more than a conqueror, and God is an awesome God. My prayer life began to look different. My Bible study began to look different. My obedience to gaining a closer relationship with God started to look different. I purchased a prayer bench for my office because I wanted a sacred place to go to God! My life started to turn around. God gave me a new assignment. And the new assignment was ME!

Walking in My Purpose and Power

I regained my purpose and power. Now I understand that I could not be where I am today without going through my struggles. I acknowledge my assignment was over at my previous employer, and God handed me a new assignment — which was ME. I stated this multiple times because we tend to make everyone else our assignment as women but ourselves. It is okay to make yourself your assignment.

Now I control my success, failures, and lessons to learn along the way. I fully embrace my journey as fast or slow as I need to go. I empower myself to pivot professionally, make decisions, and be happy. I do not earn days off; I take them when needed. I fall in love with myself daily. I show myself care and compassion daily. I give myself Grace and Mercy daily. I affirm my accomplishments daily, and I do not beat myself up for missed deadlines or mistakes. I look at mistakes as opportunities. Yes, happiness must be part of my workday. I own my day, my atmosphere, and my destiny. I remain humble and hungry.

I am a successful entrepreneur with over a million dollars in grants and opportunities. I am a motivational speaker, a two-time international best-selling author, with an amazing future because of my amazing past. I needed the past to happen because it has prepared me for my future.

Dr. Alice Prince served as the Executive Director of an American job center, where she excelled in improving the lives and prospects of the participants. Alice has been entrusted with over $25 million in government funds from a variety of programs and departments. She has been in charge of a number of federal and state contracts covering justice reform, economically empowering programs, mentorship, employment and education, workforce development, healthcare employment programs, financial literacy, and legal services.

Dr. Prince chose to work in the private sector after serving in the government for almost eleven years. She created <u>Pathways United</u>, an organization that nurtures leaders throughout the world. She has long understood the value of education when it comes to employment and raising our society's collective conscience. Her mission is to help people understand the importance of cooperation, diversity initiatives, and partnership. From a technical standpoint, Alice is known among her peers and clients as a "workforce industry specialist" for her ability to provide excellent technical support, training, and overall customer service. Dr. Prince and the Pathways United team is now blazing a trail for people of color in the bioenergy and renewable sector.

In her spare time, Dr. Prince makes sure to practice self-care while also helping others. She is a member of Delta Sigma Theta Sorority

Incorporated, serves on the board of directors for Catholic Charities, and is the host and executive director of the Good Morning Saint Louis TV show. Dr. Prince's faith propels her ahead daily. Still, she is no stranger to awards and accolades given for recognition in areas such as economic empowerment, workforce development, and being a community trailblazer.

Dr. Prince and her spouse have three children, two dogs, and one granddog. In addition to all of her business acumen, she is a well-known children's author and a harp enthusiast. She wrote a song, *Issa Vibe*, that was published on iTunes.

Dr. Prince is a two-time international best-selling author for her chapter in *Owning Your G.R.I.T.* entitled "Learning How To Kill" and her chapter, "Always Last in Line" for the Ruth Bader anthology, *Living My tRuth*.

www.dr-alice-prince.com
www.linkedin.com/in/draliceprince/

Chaundra Tatum

TRAGEDY, TRAUMA, TRIUMPH

"There is nothing quite so tragic as a young cynic because it means the person has gone from knowing nothing to believing nothing,"

— Dr. Maya Angelou

Valentine's Day 1979 began the worst and most traumatic year of my life.

Imagine being six and having no idea if your mother or unborn baby sister will live or die. Imagine being at your grandparents' home awaiting your mother's return from the store, and she doesn't return. Imagine seeing everyone leaving, rushing out of the door. That day, my mother was on the right shoulder of a street putting gas in her car. Another driver made an illegal left U-turn and smashed my mother's left leg between two bumpers. My mother was five months pregnant with my sister, and the surgeons were not sure if my mother or the baby would survive.

I turned seven the following month. I didn't have the birthday party Mom was planning before the accident. My mother was fifteen when she had me, and we pretty much grew up together. She was my best friend and hero, so I knew she would survive. In June, my mother delivered my healthy sister. She had married my sister's father, but unfortunately, a few years later, that marriage ended. This accident changed her life, and my pre-accident mother would never return.

In 1984 my mother, sister, and I moved from my grandparents' home and moved back to the projects. I was fully aware that my mother was addicted to pain pills. She needed the pills to stop the pain in her legs. If pills weren't available, any drug would do. Her accident forced me at seven to have what is now known as the hero complex, and by 14, I was a full-blown, grown woman mentally. I did what I wanted to do and willingly suffered any consequences from my decisions.

My mom was a functional drug addict. She worked the evening shift, and I watched my two sisters. I was an angry teenager full of anxiety. I began having severe psoriasis, and my face would break out if I was nervous, uncomfortable, or depressed. My only safe places were the basketball court and my grandparents' home. I thought I was doing an excellent job running my mother's household. At the tender age of fifteen, I slowly began to have my mental and physical breakdown.

My grandparents were the most caring individuals I've ever met. Even though my dad lived two miles away, my granddaddy was my protector. He was the one I called to put my mother in order. I knew his health was failing, and my grandma was the primary caregiver for him and my uncle, who is only ten months older than me. My granddaddy gave me explicit instructions on how to run my mother's household, and I followed them. Whenever I needed him, he would come regardless of his health. In October 1988, my granddaddy died. He was my protection from my mother, so once he transitioned, my trauma went from bad to worse. The leader of our tribe had passed, and my family broke down in a split second.

In 1989, I began showing signs of stress. My hair was falling out, my psoriasis was totally out of control, and I cried often. I felt I was only on this earth to watch her children, be her maid and punching bag, and neither she nor my dad noticed. This was only three months after my granddaddy died, and my grandma was grieving the love of her life. My mother's drug use had intensified, and now my aunts were abusing drugs as well. One Sunday evening in January, we had visited my aunt and were on our way home. My mother was so high that she counted her pills on the bus. I yelled at her to put them away as the bus driver and other passengers were staring at us. Once we got to our stop, I had to help her walk home. Visualize my mother in one arm, my baby sister in the other, and my other sister holding my shirt as we walked five blocks home. I cried silently, and once we got home, I went into the bathroom took out a razor blade I had glued to a toothbrush. The plan was to slit my wrist and bleed out.

God is powerful because, in that bathroom, I heard a voice that said, "Go to bed. Tomorrow will be a better day. Don't do this." I always listened to that voice. My grandma taught me about the voice of God and ensured we went to church and understood that voice. I got up and went to bed. Ironically, my grandma popped up out of the blue the next day and moved me in with her. I have no idea how she knew I was severely depressed and contemplating suicide. She never asked nor said a word except, "Chaundra, get your clothes. Today is your last day here." Later that month, my mother announced she and my two sisters were moving to Virginia for a fresh start.

> *"Stand up straight and realize who you are,
> that you tower over your circumstances."*
>
> — Dr. Maya Angelou

My grandma was one of the most beautiful human beings I had the pleasure of knowing. She loved me unconditionally and reminded me that I was an intelligent, beautiful, and graceful woman. When I moved in with her, I was defeated, and she reminded me that I was a confident, strong black woman. She also told me that my self-esteem and grace were only waiting on me to embrace them. She is the one that taught me about service and that it's our responsibility as human beings to help one another. My grandma had me and my uncle feeding the hungry at our local shelter every first Monday of the month for as long as I can remember. She challenged me to be my best self. She said, "Forgive all, and let that hurt leave your body."

She got me back on track emotionally, ensured I had doctor appointments for my psoriasis, clothes, and bi-weekly hairdresser appointments. Grandma taught me proper hygiene regimens and reminded me that my household duties were no longer my responsibility.

When I graduated from high school, I decided to leave my grandma's home in St. Louis and relocate to Virginia to attend college. Virginia is where my life's path shifted, and it marks the time my trauma began to turn into triumph.

Virginia is where I met a wonderful man who became my husband. He was in the Navy, and I will never forget the date we met — August 3, 1991. When I saw him and looked into his eyes, I knew I would marry him. Twenty-seven years later, we are still happily married, with three wonderful daughters.

At 28, I felt like this was the right time to begin a career. In high school, I had a penchant for numbers, and computers fascinated me, but I never had time to learn more about them. My first job was at Boeing as an Executive Administrator, and I worked for the Vice President of the F15 program. One day, he introduced me to Daphne and told me I would work for her. She was the one who changed my view on work ethic, my career, and provided me with focus. I was her EA for a year. I prepared all her presentations, plans, and assisted with various financial metrics. One day she stated, "You are way too smart to be my EA. You are excellent with numbers, computer hardware and software, and resolving computer system issues."

She became my mentor and encouraged me to go to college to get my certifications and degree. Daphne was so assertive about my career that she once took me in her car to four different colleges. After weeks of research, she pushed me to commit to a school and program, and I enrolled. I knew I had taken control of my career and completed my certification program quickly.

My first corporate job was at CitiGroup and my life as I knew it changed swiftly. I started at Citi as the first African-American network engineer, and my role was to manage roughly 2,100 branches and upgrade the network from analog to frame relay. That was over 20 years ago. Since then, I have relocated to grow my career path, knowledge, and skillsets. I went from a network engineer to the Director and Global Head of Development Relationship in our Internal Cloud Compute organization. In the past 18 months, I've hired and placed over 20 HBCUs graduates in Texas and bordering states.

As I look back over my life, I must admit, as Dr. Maya Angelou stated, "I've had many rainbows in my clouds." I've taken none of my personal and professional successes as mere coincidences. I know God, my Grandma Carol Jean Normal-Haynie, and my ancestors are why I overcame my tragedies and traumatic experiences. Those experiences molded me into the woman I am today and prove that with God's grace, anything is achievable.

Chaundra Tatum is a Director at Citigroup. She is the Global Head of the Development Relationship Organization within the Global Compute Services, CTI.

Chaundra has more than 22 years of experience in technology, 20 of which she has spent at Citigroup. She has a vast knowledge of regulatory and federal regulated programs, including managing billion-dollar portfolios, acquisitions, and divestitures. Chaundra currently manages the strategic relationships and drives executive alignment, product service, and marketing support, along with field and channel relationships. She also establishes and grows business and technical relationships, manages day-to-day interactions, and drives top-line revenue growth and overall market adoption for all service offerings within Global Compute.

Chaundra has an MBA, Bachelor of Science in Management and Computer Science, Associate in Arts from multiple universities, and administrative credentials from the Harvard Business School Management Program.

Chaundra is a passionate advocate of diversity and inclusion, women, and education. In her spare time, she enjoys volunteering at local charities and reading. Chaundra is a wife and proud mother of three daughters.

chaundra314@icloud.com

Gisele Marcus

From Harlem to Harvard

"Have faith in your skills, negative thoughts kill. Self-doubt will kill your dreams before others do. Doubt kills more dreams than failure ever will."

Suzy Kassem, American/Egyptian writer and philosopher

My story of overcoming is one of triumphing, teaching, and testifying that different doesn't mean deficient. While we all have biases (defined as a prejudice in favor of or against a group, a person, or a premise, usually resulting in unfair treatment), their impact can result in decisions that stall or kill dreams. Be empowered not to allow this to happen to you or those within your circle. It could be the difference between a dream having life or dying on a vine.

As a native New Yorker raised in Harlem, the odds of becoming a great success were against me. I was told that because I was a black girl from a divorced home in Harlem in the 70s, raised by my mother, I would not make it, that I would fail, and that I should settle for being an administrative assistant. There is nothing wrong with being an administrative assistant if you desire to be. However, I had career dreams and goals to move in another direction.

Despite the odds, I became a first-generation college graduate from humble beginnings, growing up in a single-parent household with a mother who pushed hard to have a better life. Harlem was a blighted community in upper Manhattan of New York City. In the 70s, it was referred to as a center of African-American culture at the intersection of underprivileged and limited opportunities. My dad was the victim of a homicide at the age of 39. He owned a bar lounge in Harlem and worked as a New York Times distribution manager. My mother was a hard-working union employee of the phone company for over 40 years.

Attending Harvard Business School was an experience that ranks high on my list of proud accomplishments. The acceptance rate is a single-digit percentage, making it an honor to be selected. During my time there, African Americans represented 5% of the class. This was not a challenge as I had grown accustomed to being the only African American, or one of a few, within corporate settings.

Nevertheless, having illustrious classmates like the godson of the President of the Ivory Coast, two sons of Stephen Covey (of the Franklin-Covey professional services organization), and a descendent of the John D. Rockefeller family (yes, I had a Rockefeller in my section) was quite impressive. It was a rigorous experience where the case study method is the instrument of learning that encapsulated reading about executives' real-life experiences. As students, we put ourselves in the protagonists' shoes and explained how we would react in such a situation—what a rich learning experience in the presence of other Type-A students.

After that, I ran an $800 million global business across 40 countries and five continents, garnered a role as Chief Operating Officer for the 10th largest revenue-generating chamber of commerce, became a trustee at Syracuse University, and have been selected as a board member of First Mid Bank & Trust, a publicly-traded bank. I have run a race that I was told would not happen.

I share my key learnings from my life's journey with you:

First, do not be afraid to apply to a top-tier educational institution or a challenging role within an organization. Never count yourself out. You do not know whether you will be accepted until you try. Remember that your competition is polishing their applications and submitting them as you ponder and potentially miss the opportunity of success. Know that your competition may not be sure of acceptance either, but they take the chance and allow the system to decide for them.

Second, do not allow others to dim your light. Be resilient about your aspirations, career, and your beliefs. Do not give in to negative stereotypes that others may present. Telling your own story allows you to define yourself. Don't allow others to tell your story. It is not their right to do so. Masterfully write your future, and do not let naysayers stand in your way.

If there is an obstacle, jump over it, move around, or go under it. As a teenager, adults told me that I would not be successful because of my race, parents' marital status, and neighborhood. If I had listened to them, I would have missed out on leading corporate assignments worldwide, including living in South Africa, running an $800 million global business, and being identified at a young age as a rising star in executive circles.

Third, remember that to whom much is given, much is required. Give your time, talent, and treasure to causes that aid the less fortunate. Why? Because many of us are one or a few actions away from having no shelter, food, clothing, or a lifestyle that is a stark contrast to the one we have today. Be good to others in need. My life from high school through today has been filled with giving. I'm currently leading a $1 million endowment campaign for students of color for the undergraduate chapter of my sorority, Delta Sigma Theta Sorority, Inc. at Syracuse University, my undergraduate alma mater.

I care about the next generation of women who look like me who may have a gap in their financial aid. I am a board member of Children & Family Institute because I care about parentless children wards of the state as I am concerned that they have opportunities to be their best selves. I serve as a Trustee at Syracuse University to give back to a university that helped form my adult self. It's good practice to be good to others.

Fourth, consider hiring a leadership coach to enhance your career development efforts. Find out if your company would invest in this effort and include it as part of your development plan. If they will not, you should. It will alter the outcomes of your career positively. I have had a Leadership Coach for the past 12 years. She has enabled me to turn on my full potential, helped me experience improved relationships with peers and leaders, and kept me mindful of watching out for obstacles and preparing for greatness in numerous transitions including, but not limited to a corporate move, an international assignment, and taking on roles of increasing responsibility. The lessons have been invaluable and life-changing, including doubling my salary over 11 years.

The greatest lesson I've learned and now promote in my teaching of diversity, equity, and inclusion is that, "different does not mean deficient," a quote often shared by my former pastor, Rev. Jeremiah A. Wright, Jr.

He first heard this quote in Dr. Janice Hale's book *Black Children: Their Roots, Culture and Learning Style* that speaks to the different learning methods between African American and European American children.

Tangentially, just because I did not fit into what society defines as a Harvard graduate, a leader of an $800 million business in a Fortune 100 company, a Trustee at a top 60 University, and an Independent Director of a $6 billion community-focused financial services network of banking centers, doesn't mean it can't happen.

Generally, society has defined black and brown people to put us into a box, limit our potential, and in some instances, hoped we did not believe in ourselves. There is fear when people who have oppressed you get concerned about you catching up to them in areas of excellence.

Long-standing inequities in education, job opportunities, and criminal justice have created an imbalance of success between races. Systematic barriers continue to hinder black and brown people from opportunity. In spite of it all, we are beginning to experience the American Dream.

Different is just different, not deficient.

Gisele Marcus is a networking expert, TEDx speaker, Harvard MBA, and first-generation college graduate. Raised in Harlem (in upper Manhattan, New York City) when the neighborhood was plagued by blight, Marcus succeeded and soared in networking and public speaking above perceived limits and all odds against her.

Marcus's expertise lies in offering practical, implementable solutions and focuses on networking, leadership, diversity, equity, and inclusion.

She has been featured in the *Huffington Post*, *Black Enterprise* magazine, the *Milwaukee Business Journal*, the *St. Louis Business Journal*, and *Good Morning St. Louis*, a business talk show on the Fox-affiliate network.

Marcus delivers knowledge, inspiration, and customization to her talks while sharing essential insights on industry trends with her audiences and clients.

Marcus serves as Professor of Practice in Diversity, Equity & Inclusion at the Olin Business School at Washington University in St. Louis, Missouri.

www.giselemarcus.com/
www.linkedin.com/in/giselemarcus/
gisele@giselemarcus.com

Patricia Bosman

What's in a Name?

Mine is a story of unconditional love, grief, faith restored, resilience, **overcoming**, and living my best life in service.

My birth name is Patricia Regenia Pearson. I was named by my Godmother, Marlene Peters, with help from the nurses at the hospital. I was taught the meaning of my first name when I was a very small child. Patricia means noble one. I began overcoming upon conception.

The story is that a doctor diagnosed my mother's pregnancy as a small abdominal mass, and as a result, prescribed pills to shrink it. However, after a few weeks, she started to feel movements in her abdomen. That's called quickening. Mother decided to see another physician. To everyone's surprise, she was pregnant with me! After too many miscarriages, she was grateful for the blessing of another pregnancy. She desperately wanted to have a daughter this time. Mother promised God that this child's life would be lived in service to Him and assured Him that if I were to be a girl, I would be virtuous, of good character, and a living sacrifice to His blessings, grace, and mercy.

Over the years, I heard that story many times, and please believe, my mother meant every word of her promise. I tried my best to live up to her vow. I can imagine how heartbroken she must have been when she noticed that I had a tiny bump in my abdomen. I was sixteen years old and only in high school, and I was going to be a mother. Although a little embarrassed and perhaps disappointed, my parents loved me unconditionally. They continued to provide support, shelter, and grace in exchange for the promise that I would finish high school. I delivered Larry Antione Pearson, a beautiful 7 pounds, 6-ounce baby boy. Two weeks later, I headed back to high school.

At 8:30 a.m. on March 31, 1996, on a cloudy day, the phone rang. Because the call came early on a Sunday morning, I checked my Caller ID before answering. It was my mother, Charlean Pearson. She was a mighty prayer warrior, and I believed as near an angel as any woman could be. I loved my mother deeply and admired her for many reasons, but especially because of how she leaned into her faith at all times. When times were good, God was blessing, and during not-so-great times, according to her, He was teaching life's lessons.

As the years moved on, Momma and I became more like two old girlfriends rather than mother and daughter. We often chatted, made up our own corny jokes, and giggled like schoolgirls if the devil got into us when someone was unnecessarily bossy or mean. We were close. So close that I often answered her calls by saying, "Hey girl, what's going on?" Gleefully, with certainty, she would respond, "Girl, folks died today who never died before," and we would crack up laughing! That was her way of keeping me abreast of my old neighborhood's happenings and reminding me to put the funeral dates of elderly persons on my calendar. It was important not to miss any opportunity to pay respects to the royalty of Hadley Township. Located in Richmond Heights, MO, our community was the last historically African American neighborhood in Central St. Louis County, neighboring Clayton, MO.

March 31, 1996, was going to be different. I answered the phone in my typical fashion by saying, "Hey, girl, what's going on?"

Momma didn't respond in her usual playful way. The words I heard would change my life, my view of problems, and how I show up in the world forever. Through uncontrollable sobbing, Momma said, "He's gone."

The next voice was that of a Richmond Heights, MO, police officer. He determined that Momma wasn't communicating very well and that my father was in apparent shock. The officer took the phone from her and said, "I'm sorry to inform you that your son, Larry A. Pearson, has been taken to the St. Louis City Coroner's Office."

Confused, I said, "What in the world are you talking about, sir? That doesn't make any sense because the coroner's office is where they take dead people."

I thought this must be a dream, but it was not. A few days later, I buried Larry Antione Pearson Sr. He was 21 years old, murdered at a party after a fistfight by a 19-year-old acquaintance who had purchased a handgun off the street two weeks prior. Lives, spirits, and hearts were changed forever on that day, ours, a black family, and the other one, white. Two mothers were thrust into despair to experience unfathomable loss. The shooter would be convicted and sentenced to two life sentences.

The pain and agony of losing a child was unlike anything I could ever have imagined. Inconceivable, almost indescribable, and agonizing. Months filled with dark days and foggy nights separated my spirit from my body. Living was hard, and I did so almost in the abstract. Instead, I decided only to exist. No peace or joy, just existing.

I developed a deep line from the fixed grimace that I wore on my face upon my brow. How could something like this happen to my family? I searched for answers. Why him, why me, why us? "Was God somehow angry with me," I asked? Well, what more could I have done to fulfill my mother's promise to him? Hadn't I already been through enough lessons? I had overcome the challenges of being a teen mother, learned to stand up for my child's existence, and shared my narrative before anyone could attempt to define or label me. Those who share the teen mom experience can surely relate. Always polite, respectful, and somewhat soft-spoken, I could go on the defense with the force of a velvet hammer, if any dared to call us fast or socially stigmatize us in any way. We were children, but we chose to keep our babies. To the haters, I asked, "What harm have our choices done to you?"

After Larry was stolen away, talks with God continued and went something like, "God, I don't understand how you let something like this happen. We followed all your rules. We are a Christian family who attends church. We are married, college-educated, donate to favorite charities, and live the best version of the so-called American dream. God, I made tremendous strides in life by using a childhood lapse in judgment as fuel to show that something good can come from any situation."

As far as I was concerned, I delivered on the promise. Although during a very frank conversation with Him, I admitted that our lives were as imperfect as any other family. At times, I tried to negotiate a rollback of time, arguing with God and providing rationale around the reasons death shouldn't visit my family's house. I would debate with him by saying, "I worked long hours to ensure the children had a nice house, the latest sneakers, and video games, and in doing so, I sacrificed little league baseball, basketball, and football games. I did all of that to get Larry to manhood, and you take him away. How could you? God, are you listening?" I could not hear Him. So, I did what hurt humans do. I got super mad and cast my faith to the proverbial curve. I closed my eyes, heart, and head, then folded my arms and quit God. Done!

Curled in the fetal position after one of many anxiety attacks, I heard the sobering voice of my 13-year-old daughter, Erica, who said, "Momma, I am still here, and you have to live for me." She was also feeling tremendous grief and desperately needed my attention. Then Larry's two-year-old son, Little Larry, grabbed my chin with his tiny fingers and asked, "Are you crying about my daddy? I'm your son now, and I will never leave you". The three of us lay huddled together on the floor, consoling and loving one another. It was at that moment that Momma's teachings came to mind. During the most difficult times, she said that God is no respecter of persons. Also, at that moment, I realized that I still believed and that God had much bigger issues to tackle than my anger. He had been true to His word as He had held me close in His arms through the funeral and trial and had given me strength and a clear mind to function professionally after returning to work. He heard me, and His spirit was always present. Later that day, I walked outside to the mailbox. I noticed that the fog seemed to have been lifted to give way to the bright sunlight. Mine and the neighbor's grass seemed greener, and I saw flowers in my pot. My perspective returned clearly, and I could answer my own question. "How could this happen to me?" The answer was, "Why not me?" The worst that could happen has already happened, and I survived. I decided to live, lead in the spirit of service, and view every challenge as an opportunity for growth.

After a distinguished career in Corporate America, I chose to begin a new life of servant leadership in the nonprofit sector. In memoriam to my wonderful parents, Charlean and Willie B. Pearson, Sr., I volunteer as Board Chairman at a community nonprofit that provides a safe, comfortable, wholesome, and stimulating environment for the aged and persons with special needs. Over the years, I have continued to serve marginalized communities to volunteer work for various nonprofits in the St. Louis Metropolitan Area.

God always has a plan for our lives. An inaccurate medical diagnosis of a small abdominal mass, a tiny belly bump on a 16-year-old teen girl, death, grief, and spiritual rebirth, all to provide me with the tools of a noble person: humility, gratefulness, resiliency, and unwavering faith in GOD and the spirit of humankind in preparation for the continuation of my journey.

I am overcoming and living my best life, in spite of...

Patricia Bosman is a strategic, operational, and entrepreneurial executive with 30 years of experience across nonprofit and corporate sectors.

She enjoyed a distinguished career as a leader in the telecommunications industry. For more than 20 years, she managed domestic and international information technology initiatives for AT&T, Inc., formerly SBC Corporation.

Lauded as a natural connector and peacemaker, she is skilled at collaborating social constructs, communicating persuasively, and problem-solving with ease. Patricia has an unwavering commitment to supporting individuals in marginalized communities and has a passion for building strong relationships with everyone from clients, community partners, and everyone in between — always with a healthy dose of integrity, adaptability, and respect.

She holds a Bachelor of Arts in Marketing and a Master of Arts in Management and Leadership from Webster University. She is a graduate of the CORO Women in Leadership program, and she has earned multiple professional certifications. Patricia was also the Eureka! STEM Manager and Center Director for Girls Incorporated of St. Louis for more than three years.

Patricia is the current Executive Director of The Haven of Grace. The organization serves pregnant and homeless women. The Haven of Grace provides a safe, nurturing home, educational programs, and long-term support for mother and child. Founded in faith, they instill hope, dignity and the pride of independence, one family at a time.

Patricia is married to jazz artist and composer Dwayne Bosman, one-half of the Legendary Bosman Twins. They have a blended family of 7 children and a growing number of grandchildren.

www.linkedin.com/in/patriciarbosman/
www.bosmanwilliamsphoenix.com/
www.facebook.com/patricia.reedboswell/

Shaire Lynnette Duncan, ABD, Ed.S

It was Necessary

Pain is prescribed. It is not punishment, and it does not need our permission. It does not care if you are wealthy or poor. There is a purpose in our pain. Nothing worth birthing can occur without pain. There is power in our pain. Innovation and creativity can't happen without the stages and phases of pain. Growing up, belonging, connecting, and finding my voice was a struggle. I fought at school and in the neighborhood. I was labeled the "angry black student" because of misplaced anger and frustration; I exhibited aggressive behaviors.

The core of my anger and frustration came from home responsibilities and expectations. Some of those responsibilities consisted of caring for my siblings and first cousins. I grew up feeling robbed of my childhood. We grew up in a two-bedroom house with about thirteen children and three adults. By my early teens, I had witnessed more than my share of traumatic experiences. This included the death of my three-month-old nephew, the murder of my cousin, and a house fire that resulted in us moving out of our home and moving in with my aunt's friend. Those childhood experiences contributed to how I viewed the world and shaped how I saw myself.

Childhood Trauma (Fatherless Daughter)

I am a fatherless daughter and it impacted how I selected men in my life. The only male figures in my life were my uncles and grandfather. I saw my father three times in my entire life. The first time was when I was in third grade. The second time I was in fifth grade, and the third time I was in eighth grade. My last encounter with my father was at his funeral. In addition to his death, I was also devastated because I found out that he had adopted his wife's daughter. I was like, "WOW, what is wrong with me? Was I not good enough to be your daughter and to be a part of your life? Why did you have to adopt a daughter when you already had your own biological daughter?" My stepsister cried the entire funeral. She, too, was devastated and nonchalant at the funeral. She was staring at me in disbelief and barely said anything to me because she had just learned that I was our father's biological daughter.

As I sat at my father's funeral, I thought to myself, "Why are you upset? You had support. Your father lived in the house with you." My heart dropped when they presented my father's flag to my brother. After all, I was the oldest. They had our father all their lives; I didn't have him at all. I cried when I made it home from the funeral because I had suppressed my emotions during his funeral services. When my daughter was younger, I still remember weeping and praying to God that she would never experience what I had experienced as a fatherless daughter.

Physical Abuse/Domestic Violence

During my early twenties, I dated a man who was mentally and physically abusive. I met him at a club on the east side. He was in a relationship with a woman, and they shared a child. He had also fathered another child outside of his household. We had so much fun, and I believed the chemistry was authentic. I was the woman with a job and an education. I was convinced that he would leave his girlfriend, we would become a couple, and get married. His girlfriend and his other baby momma knew of me, and I knew of them. Later, I found out that he was lying to all of us to get what he wanted.

Then, the physical abuse started. He would pick arguments that escalated to physical altercations. Several days went by, he would call and apologize, and I would forgive him. This cycle would be repeated many times. We were at a club one Saturday night, and he became jealous. He picked up a beer bottle and hit me in the head because I was out on the dance floor. I ended up with stitches on my forehead. This left a scar that reminds me of the poor choices and judgment in the past. You would think that was the end of the story. Nope! Weeks later, we reconnected, I forgave him, and the saga continued. I repeated the behavior of the women in my family who settled for being the side piece. It left me feeling broken and bruised.

Marital Pain

Two weeks before my wedding date, I prayed and asked God to reveal if he was the man for me. Because he was jobless, our families felt we should postpone our nuptials. There was a lot of noise and chatter centered around whether we should or shouldn't get married.

During my marriage, I existed in chaos and lost my true essence. I was overeating, overcompensating, and compromising my worth and value as a woman out of fear. Fear of being alone. Fear of what people would say. Fear of the noise and chatter from outsiders. Fear of rearing my children alone.

The divorce was gut-wrenching, devastating, and felt like losing a loved one to death. It was also a reminder of another failure and disappointment. I had thrown myself into the marriage, only to end up divorced.

After the divorce, depression and anxiety crept in and almost took me out. I masked the pain during and after the divorce. This added another layer of trauma that I had to unpack and heal. The depression was getting the best of me. I realized that I could no longer run from the pain by masking the traumatic experiences that occurred in my childhood. Without being aware of it, I had picked up some unhealthy parenting strategies and beliefs that I had learned from my childhood and inflicted them on my children. As the breadwinner, I attended school full-time and worked full-time, yet I was emotionally unavailable to my children. I wanted to make life better for my children, and I did not want them to encounter the hardships I had when I was a child. My desire for them was to be in a stable home environment filled with faith, love, support, and compassion.

The trauma caused me to overcompensate with my children, jobs, family, friends, etc. Because I did not know who I was, my worth, or my value as a Black woman, I struggled with naming what I wanted and needed. I gave consistently without considering the cost of overcompensating and failed to stand up for what was important to me. It was vital for me to establish boundaries and call out what I wanted and needed. I learned to be okay with saying "No!" (No is a complete sentence). I refrained from engaging in passive-aggressive and people-pleasing behaviors. Leaning in and doing the work was critical to my journey of removing the masks of shame, guilt, and abandonment, no matter the cost.

Being a mother, school leader, and student working on my dissertation made me question my beliefs about not being good enough, being a good writer, and keeping the program going. I spent time and money obtaining all of the degrees and accomplishments to mask the pain and trauma of my past, not realizing that those accomplishments and degrees could not take away the hurt, pain, and experiences of my past. They only became a temporary fix until the next trigger.

There is power in storytelling. I disrupt family pathology through storytelling that prevents us from being our truest and authentic selves. This disruption and pain were necessary to change the trajectory of future generations in my family. I know all too well about being stuck, stagnant, and living from the neck down.

It Was Necessary

I am not my past, nor am I what happened to me. I am not my childhood trauma. My past experiences and trauma do not define who I am. They are a part of my *Becoming* journey. I am responsible for knowing my worth, joy, and happiness. I had to own my healing and tell myself that it was okay to begin again. It is okay to have a new beginning.

It was important for me to lean in and reflect to find out where the pain and emotions were coming from, so I would not continue inflicting my pain on my village, especially my children. It was important for me to speak truth to power regarding issues of the heart. Standing in my truth and owning my story provided me with a greater sense of self-awareness regarding my feelings and emotions. In addition, it gave me the ability to articulate life situations and circumstances that prevented me from showing up authentically. I was surviving instead of thriving. I had to get out of my head and get out of my way!

Throughout my journey of overcoming, I have tapped into the power source! My faith is the power source for me. Underneath the pain was power, passion, perseverance, joy, compassion, empathy, untapped gifts, and talents waiting to be discovered. I realized that if I continued doing the same things I have always done, I would get what I have always gotten. The disruption was necessary.

> *"Learn to get in touch with the silence within yourself and know that everything in life has a purpose. This includes our pain. There are no mistakes, no coincidences, all life events are blessings given to us to learn from."*
>
> –Dr. Elisabeth Kübler-Ross

It was necessary! I am an overcomer!

Shaire Lynnette Duncan, ABD, Ed.S is a K-8 middle school leader for St. Louis Public Schools. Born and educated in St. Louis, she has made it her mission to be the change she wants to see in public education. She holds multiple advanced degrees and certifications, including a Master's of Education in Secondary Curriculum & Instruction, a Master's of Education in Special Education, both from the University of Missouri-St. Louis; and Educational Specialist in Educational Leadership, through Webster University.

Shaire is a currently a candidate for the Doctorate of Education in Educational Leadership at Missouri Baptist University, completing her dissertation on "Educational Equity-Access-Inclusion," which focuses on giving students a voice in their education and making sure those voices are heard.

Shaire is the mother of three children and likes comfy hoodies, colorful tennis shoes, and good music. She's the founder of Bridging the Gap 4 Youth by Youth, supporting young people exploring careers in education, science, technology, the arts, engineering, and mathematics.

Her favorite quote is, "Not everything that is faced can be changed, but nothing can be changed until it is faced." –James Baldwin

www.ShaireDuncan.com
Shaire@ShaireDuncan.com
www.twitter.com/chosen0128
www.instagram.com/chosen_0128/
www.facebook.com/shaired1
www.linkedin.com/in/shaire-l-duncan-ed-s-44612979/

Marshá Reynolds

Overcoming My Perspective

None of us see things as they are. We see things as we are.

I grew up an only child raised by a single mom, and yes, my dad was very present in my life. I loved my childhood. I felt loved, protected, and happy. Like most single children, you can imagine my vivid imagination. I spent hours alone entertaining myself with a variety of activities. This will give my age away, but back then, for hours, I could be found in my room, absorbed in reading all of my Sweet Pickles books or found thumbing through the volumes of Encyclopedia Britannica my mom spent a small fortune on for my education. Sometimes I'd write or talk to myself about who knows what. I'd sit alone for hours living in my imagination. Within my mind, I mapped out the most wonderful life for myself.

I have a friend that will tease me to this day, saying, "You are always in your own world." I think to myself, "Yes, because that's where all the black girl magic happens first — in my own world." I remember as a girl, I'd sit in my grandparents' front room parlor at my grandfather's desk for hours. I'd pretend I was a business owner or a bank manager, and I'd solve big problems for my staff. I'd visualize myself being a speaker, a mother, a professor, a rockstar in any given field. I could sit at that desk for hours, cultivating my ability to imagine and visualize myself doing the most amazing things. It was an escape, a glimpse, if you will, into my future. I could go anywhere without limits. I later would understand that my ability and skill to direct my imagination using visualization would be an extremely powerful tool for my future. It would set the tone for how I approached life and showed up daily.

As I matured and grew into a young woman, my friends would tease me. They'd say, "What are you laser focused on and checking off your list now"? I thought it was strange. Didn't everyone make a list of daily goals? It was just second nature for me. Step 1: Make a plan, Step 2: Visualize the outcome, Step 3: Take Action towards realizing my goal.

Goal-setting just comes naturally for me. After all, whenever I sat at my grandfather's desk, my secretary would transfer calls to me, and I'd quickly push a few buttons on granddad's vintage adding machine calculator with the computing loud paper roll sound and poof...

Just like that, crisis averted!.

Now don't get me wrong, my life was not just a conveyor belt of constant wins, triumphs, and mountain-high experiences. As a kid, I dealt with molestation at the hands of different family members during various stages of my life. I've witnessed close domestic violence experiences and wondered, "Am I safe here tonight?" Unfortunately, sometimes no matter how closely we try to protect each other, things can still happen in families.

Growing into womanhood, I, like many women, fell into a cycle of unfruitful dating scenarios that would leave me in search of my true love. I found myself in my 30s, coasting along and doing okay.

I was surviving, but that's all. One day during a team-building event at work, that realization hit me like a ton of bricks. I was surviving, but how would I make it to thrive in life?

I remembered that little girl who spent hours realizing her hopes and dreams within her imagination. I began to search for that daydreamer in me who would visualize the best outcome and go after it. Right then and there, I decided to make a change. I needed to change my outlook and my focus. That day I adopted a word that I'd use as a constant reminder for what I was going after. I chose the word THRIVE. The definition of thrive is" to do well and be successful, healthy, or strong." I'd repeat the word "thrive" hundreds of times daily in my mind, saying it aloud, writing it on sticky notes, really whatever it took. Everything had to line up with that word, and if it did not serve me or my mission, I let it go. I'd see myself living out its attributes, and I fully believed I was an irresistible magnet for all that belonged to me by my divine right.

I just had to thrive but, how could I THRIVE daily? Overnight, I'd awakened that child inside of me and unlocked her drive and potential. Within the next year, I found myself happier, loving my career, and in a beautiful relationship headed for marriage.

Not long after, I had a fairytale wedding surrounded by friends and loved ones, and before I knew it, with work and life blossoming, a year had passed. Then, a new desire would begin to swell in my heart. That tiny swell that only a baby could fill, and in a little under two years, the girl that found herself reaching goals and checking boxes looked around and was surrounded by calendars, checklists, and thermometer charts covering the bathroom floor. I was in disbelief. I was struggling to recall and count up the times? Was this miscarriage eight or nine? I searched my memory, but the pain and shock blurred the dates. I WAS DEVASTATED. I was broken into tiny pieces, angered by this betrayal again, and now I had no reason to peel myself up off of the bathroom floor this time. I was consumed with grief. I'd lost this baby after nine weeks, and I COULD NOT BREATHE!

I eventually had to leave the bathroom, but to do what? I couldn't watch TV because every commercial was about babies, families, or mommy products. I cringed at the thought of social events because people can be so insensitive sometimes. They are not meaning to inflict harm but asking questions about when a person will have children when you don't know their struggles is a huge trigger. Some days when asked, I wanted to say, "I have children, they are just all in heaven!!" Maybe that would get people to stop asking me when I was going to have a child. I knew that was just the grief responding, but I was truly at a loss.

I still had to find the will to keep going, refusing to allow the pain to paralyze me. When IFV failed, we tried other paths. The costs climbed into huge financial scales with no guarantees. How do you deal with the defeat and the financial devastation it causes? The doctors kept saying everything is fine with our bodies but had no real answers.

Sis, I tell you, the fertility journey can be lonely. The isolation and fear are enough to break you and all you've worked to build. People take so much for granted, and it's hard to watch sometimes, but I knew I had to remain steadfast and true to myself.

Sometimes you have to turn your back on the world and forge your path to make it all make sense. I found myself in a "REAL" place. That place every woman must travel alone. That place where she must sit down and say to herself, "Either you are going to die here, or get up and live. Either you are going to sit here and gain 50 pounds, or you are going to go to the gym today."

You say to yourself, "You have two choices; either you are going to hate this circumstance, or you are going to get serious about living with an attitude of gratitude for all of it." That includes gratitude even for the things sent for you to endure.

I began to remember that little girl with the limitless imagination sitting at her grandfather's desk that would flood her mind with possibilities, not problems. That girl was never concerned with the details or where the road led. She solved problems in the blink of an eye with the click of the calculator. And she was never worried about what anyone thought of her. She was fearless. Before I knew it and without really trying, I woke up one day and felt the universe pushing me towards expansion and abundance, pushing me towards that little girl inside me. The more I opened up to receive, the more I received.

A normal day was far from normal anymore. I began to place noticeable value on my daily routines and rituals. Simple things like bathing, cooking, cleaning, journaling, meditating and eating less takeout were like little opportunities to tell my body and surroundings that I was grateful for them. I began to look for all the joyful moments I could find. Joyful moments like driving to work and noticing the sky looking especially blue. Or turning on the shower water to the perfect temperature without even trying. Or that moment when I get the best parking spot on the lot. I looked for little pockets of joyful moments that made me happy, and in return, those joyful moments began to look for and chase after me. I asked myself how I could go out of my way to show gratitude for everything around me, everyone around me, and every circumstance — even the undesirable ones.

Gratitude just felt better than the disappointment did.

See, the disappointment didn't serve me, so I let it go. Striving to live in a constant state of gratitude will change your perspective, and in doing so, you will change. Where your energy goes, energy will flow, and I learned that the universe will instinctively give you MORE of what you focus on. So, I focused on being grateful, and the universe gave me more things to be grateful for.

I understand now that perspective is fluid, and it can easily be manipulated. It's not about seeing things as THEY ARE because, as I said, we will only see things as WE ARE.

I am still on the journey to being a better, more grateful human being. I still have negative thoughts and responses, and I am also grateful for them because they remind me to shift and pivot my energy and perspective in those moments. I love where I am, and I am so eager for what's coming next. I overcame my perspective and decided I was in control of what I saw.

Overcome your perspective, and who knows what you might be able to see!

Marshá Reynolds: Overcoming My Perspective

Marshá L. Reynolds is a proud native of St. Louis, Missouri. Educationally trained in organizational studies, she has over 20 years of experience in Human Resources, Leadership Development, Initiative Management, and Program Facilitation.

Marshá has a passion for serving the youth of the disparate communities of her hometown. She is currently the Executive Director of The Sophia Project, a not-for-profit mentoring program for high-school girls. She is on a mission to educate and empower at-risk young women growing up in today's ever-changing, ego-focused, and media-driven world.

Marshá graduated from the University of Missouri-St. Louis, where she earned her Bachelor's Degree in Communications. She is employed as a Human Resources Executive in the food & nutritional healthcare industry with a concentration in short-term healthcare management.

Having a zeal for life and an appreciation for all things travel and exploration, Marshá loves rich cultural mixes, live music, art festivals, and unique dining experiences.

She and her husband never miss the opportunity to embrace all of the new cultural vibes during their traveling adventures.

Marshá believes that gratitude is short for a great attitude and having gratitude helps us see what is there instead of what is not.

www.facebook.com/marsha.williams.39501
www.instagram.com/shealwayswinning100/
www.linkedin.com/in/marshareynolds/
Mreynolds@thesophiaproject.org
williml08@gmail.com

Marion "Rossi" Kunney

My Stones are Now Diamonds

    I am a Southerner from Yazoo City, Mississippi, a small town, northwest of Jackson. At one time, my cooking and eating habits were typical of many people born and raised below the Mason Dixon. For instance, tea is not desirable until the sugar content makes your head swim. Reared in the 1960s, I am sure everything I ate until age fifteen was deep-fried, smothered, or covered in gravy. They say even our breast milk flows with the aroma of warm buttered biscuits. My roots are anchored in the belief that every bite of soul food cooked must be consumed, and you must eat until overwhelming tiredness embraces you. To do anything less is disrespectful.

    I am proud of the abundance of flavor, accompanied by the history and culture of a Southern diet. On occasion, I smile at the memory of my mother and grandmother cooking apple and pecan pies that makes me appreciate even more the love they put in every meal. I recall my mother rushing home from work to fry chicken so flavorful that the smell would reach my bus stop a block away. I also remember watching my grandmother cleaning fish and canning fresh fruits and vegetables that would last throughout the winter. The tin can filled with tea cakes that my grandmother sent to my college dorm always caused a frenzy amongst my friends, and they begged for at least one. Meals were prepared with love and much boasting about the best potato salad or whose collard greens were so good that you could eat them without cornbread.

The recipes or lack thereof (because some dishes are just "in the wrist") were passed down from generation to generation. And while many of my fondest memories growing up are smothered and battered in grandma's gravy, it took decades for me to overcome both my addiction to fatty foods and the belief that I had to own the health issues that come with it as well.

I prepare many of these dishes for my family, with healthier changes that I don't believe would get my grandmother's approval. I say this because my 84-year-old mother still thinks it's a travesty that I don't batter and smother enough. However, she rarely uses fatty meats to season her food anymore, and she recently purchased an air fryer. She's owned it for several months and keeps promising to use it. We both now know there are health concerns associated with consuming high-fat meals every day without exercise.

Speak Over Me

The first thing I noticed about our youngest at birth was his eyebrows. I had seen them on most men in my husband's family. Our elders never needed a swab of saliva to identify lineage in the past. That child is the spitting image of her grandmother, or he walks just like his daddy, they would say. Over and over, we've heard these phrases, often accompanied by a grin or smile. These terms of endearment solidified your place in a family. However, some words spoken over a child rest in the tiny recesses of their psyche, then manifest negatively in adulthood.

In addition to enjoying memorable meals, the adults in my life would casually say that I would grow up to resemble a close relative. "You gone look just like your aunt when you grow up" is something I heard on numerous occasions. I remember being excited because she was one of my more colorful relatives. Tall and stout, I loved the way she walked and marveled at her use of profanity. We may have referred to her as "big-boned." When she entered the house, her voice and laugh reverberated around the room, captivating everyone within earshot. I can still envision her large brown hands and thick fingers adorned with numerous beautiful rings. I inhaled who she was and felt honored that I would look like her, and one day someone would surely idolize me in the same way. Although my family was speaking about my likeness and destiny, they were not cognizant of what I would have to consume to mimic my aunt's size and stature.

At that time, no one spoke of generational curses or diseases replicated throughout our ancestry. Consequently, at age 35, 5'8, and 200 pounds, I found myself shopping at stores that catered to larger women believing that this was my destiny. After all, this was spoken into me as an adolescent.

Finding My Tribe

In my twenties, my roommate and I would hit the gym religiously in stylish workout gear and a full face of makeup — lipstick included. Everything had to coordinate perfectly. And to reward ourselves after our "workout," we would hit a fast-food drive-thru. We embraced the concept that you can consume whatever you want if you exercise regularly. Neither of us was raised with the idea that diet and exercise were part of your "normal" lifestyle, so we never connected the dots that these two were vital in extending our lives.

In my thirties, I purchased numerous workout videos to use in the comforts of my home while possessing memberships to multiple gyms all over Atlanta. Although I was a faithful member, I was equally committed to a diet leading to obesity and chronic diseases.

Overcoming the destiny assigned to me didn't become my reality until I was in my forties. Although I had been altering our family recipes to create healthier options, I struggled to maintain a healthy lifestyle at 196 pounds. I started experiencing pain in my knees and ankles due to the extra weight I was carrying, but I still didn't have the willpower to move in another direction. I was secretly preparing for high blood pressure, which plagued my family and most African Americans for generations.

I needed a new voice, and not the memory of my aunt, to guide me. I needed inspiration.

That inspiration came when I saw a picture of my friend Angela on Facebook. Although we had been friends since the third grade, I hadn't seen her in several years. Angela was standing next to her son at his high school graduation and could have easily passed as a graduate herself. She was glowing. Her skin was smooth, and she appeared to have gained little to no weight since college with perfectly toned, muscular legs and arms. My first thought was, *"What is this witchcraft, and how can I join the coven?"* I immediately called to get the scoop. Angela shared that she had invested time building a network of like-minded women determined to make fitness their "normal."

I knew I needed to find my squad. I needed to be selfish and thankful for the ability to move. I was on the hunt for a resource that could push, motivate, and hold me accountable when I wanted to give up. But what weighed heavier on my mind was this thought, "If I move, maybe someone else will move as well."

There are times when you know the path you're on is destined for you. One week after my conversation with Angela, I met a dynamic group of women ranging in age from late '20s to early '60s. They became my squad. At least three days a week, we met with an excellent trainer at 6:00 in the morning. The classes stretched me beyond anything you could imagine doing, especially at 46 years of age. There were days I cried on my way to a session. The workouts were challenging and painful. I wanted to give up on numerous occasions. My reaction was common for many people when beginning a life-altering journey. However, I always felt I could accomplish what was assigned to me. I had a group of strong-willed women pushing and believing in me. I was not alone.

Be Selfish

Most people are raised to share. You tell your kids, *"Stop hoarding your toys or let your siblings have a chance to play the game."* However, there are times when we need to be selfish. I believe in digging my heels in and fighting for things that mean the most to me. I am protective about the energy in my home and value the positive relationships I have. I had to learn to apply this same principle to a healthier existence. My body, my temple, is a blessing, and I no longer allow the enemy (or family history) to conquer.

Now, at 166 pounds, I'm not at risk of diabetes, high cholesterol, or blood pressure, and I look forward to a positive annual health report. For years, my doctor has bragged about my results and tells me I should "bottle what I'm doing." But the best part of my journey is the people who see me and decide to start moving. I enjoy hearing from followers who have changed their paths because of an encouraging word, a healthy dish I've posted, or a new workout.

The words spoken into me as a child, although with loving intentions, were tiny stones of a broken destiny. I had to apply an extreme amount of pressure whenever I wanted to give up. Maintaining a healthy lifestyle is still a challenge, however, those stones are beginning to shine like diamonds. The brilliance began to grow when I found a network of women determined to motivate and excel. I needed to quiet the voice in my head that told me I was not worthy of taking a different path. I had to be strong and selfish enough to ensure the diseases that ran through my family for years would "run out" with me.

Marion "Rossi" Kunney is the founder of MACSquad by Rossi, where she motivates women to pursue a rational and reasonable approach to a healthier lifestyle. However, getting stronger, more fit, and healthier wasn't always a priority for her.

After moving to Atlanta in 1989, she began a 26-year career at Verizon Wireless with increasing roles in Finance, Fraud, and Customer Service. Although managing fraud losses of approximately $35 million and a budget of $20 million was quite challenging and fulfilling, at times, she always felt that her true purpose rested in serving the community. In July 2017, when she could retire, Rossi took the leap and parted ways with Verizon.

MACSquad by Rossi encourages motivation, accountability, and change to a fantastic squad of women. As an accountability resource, she provides unique tools to help women choose and move daily. Rossi displays her passion by blogging and sharing videos and healthy meals through various social media platforms, including Twitter, Instagram, Facebook, and Podcasting.

She and her husband, Christopher, enjoy an empty nest in Atlanta, GA, where they raised two amazing boys, Brian and Jordan.

www.facebook.com/MACSquad-by-Rossi-109464387089364/
www.facebook.com/marion.kunney
www.instagram.com/iamrossikunney
www.linkedin.com/in/marion-rossi-kunney-53873b21/
Still in the Game with Rossi Kunney Podcast

Charlotte Hammond

Strength to Overcome

Believe it or not, I lived a real-life fairy tale. I married the man of my dreams, had the wedding of my dreams, the family, and the life only dreams could describe. I couldn't have asked for more. I couldn't have foreseen a heart attack would snatch my husband at the age of 37 away after only 4 ½ years of marriage with a newborn. No way was he gone!

It was impossible to believe my fairy tale was over. There were so many emotions and thoughts. This must be a horrible dream; what's going to happen now? Did I miss signs that something was wrong? I'm a first-time mom with a 9-month-old and how will I raise her alone? I broke down in tears. I wasn't sure if anything prepared me at the age of 32 to be a widow, but somehow, God calmed me and gave me strength after this tragedy, that even now I cannot explain.

Our love story started at a traditional small Baptist church where we both grew up. I was active there, singing in the choir, serving on the usher board, and attending Sunday school. My parents were pretty strict, so most of my social life revolved around high school activities and church. A very handsome young man returned to church from a short stint in the Navy named Horace Jones. Horace was five years my senior, so I never paid much attention to him in the church before. By the time he returned,

I was 16, and he was 21. Of course, at 16, I was not the little girl he remembered before leaving for the Navy.

There was an immediate attraction brewing. I would sneak and talk on the phone with him growing closer and closer. One day he stopped by my house. Again I'm 16, and he is 21. My mom, the disciplinarian, stopped him at the door and said, "Charlotte will not be dating you." Then closed the door in his face. My parents thought he was too old and had experienced too much. Despite my parents' disapproval, we continued to talk on the phone, growing closer, and would periodically see each other outside of the church. Our relationship continued to be platonic and developed into a beautiful friendship and love. Before leaving for college, he once told me that he wanted me to experience life because you never marry your first serious relationship.

Horace and I continued to, respectfully as friends, see each other during holiday and summer breaks building an incredible bond. Having that platonic relationship and building on our Christian beliefs, respectful friendship, and love for each other organically kept us tied to each other. We each continued to engage in separate relationships after graduating from college yet still saw each other every Sunday at church. It was sometimes strange because he was very attractive, and we still had somewhat of a cat and mouse relationship.

I didn't act on it. Maybe I thought I had possibly grown past that relationship. Did I forget to say that Horace was very handsome, sexy, and smart? He was very much the "ladies' man." Fast forward almost five or six years - Horace had a baby with another woman. That was a game-changer in my mind. I thought we most likely would never have an opportunity to have a serious relationship. Well, not true. Horace made every effort to make the relationship work with his daughter's mom, even buying a home and living together. Their relationship didn't work out.

That magnetic attraction brought us back together again. We started seeing each other, and it almost felt like a fairy tale. It was a whirlwind for both of us. I was 26, and he was 31. Age was no longer a factor, and the bond that brought us together just grew stronger. I knew that it was serious when I took him to meet my friends and sorority sisters from Ole Miss. I wanted them to know about this guy and see how he interacted with them. They loved him, which I knew they would.

Again, fast forward into this whirlwind. Horace and I started talking about marriage. We had only been dating a year but had been friends since I was 16. The love of my life asked me to marry him almost a year into dating. We didn't want to wait, so we planned one of the biggest weddings in less than four months. Again, a fairy-tale wedding with my friend, confidant, spiritual partner and love. We had over 600 people attend, with all the bells and whistles on October 29, 1994. We started like most couples saving for a dream home. So we lived in a townhouse our first year of marriage. I started my professional career as an accountant, and Horace was an account manager with Lucent Technologies.

My step-daughter, Carly, was also a part of this new union as we grew as a family. We were both doing well in our careers and growing closer and closer. A year later, we purchased a beautiful fixer-upper in St. Louis' dream area — in the Central West End. This was a 3,000 square foot-plus home, three stories, and in one of the city's most affluent areas. We gradually made repairs and cosmetic improvements, building a beautiful home.

We opened our own dry-cleaning business about a year or two later. We kept our full-time jobs and eventually had a chain of dry cleaners. Horace and I believed in business ownership, so we were evenly yoked in many areas. Almost 3 ½ years into our marriage, we found out we would be parents. We were extremely happy, and so was our family.

In September 1998, our beautiful baby girl was born, and we named her Haley. We struggled with finding adequate daycare for me to return to work after six weeks. Someone recommended a lady who was willing to come to the house, and she was wonderful and an unbelievable blessing.

> Matthew 6:8, *"for your Father, knoweth what things ye have need of, before ye ask him."*

Our cleaners were doing well, careers going great, our family was expanding, and we were feeling blessed. Then, the nightmare came. On June 6, while sleeping, Horace suddenly fell over on me. I immediately sat up and cut the light on to see that he was having a heart attack.

While we were dating, Horace had been hospitalized with chest pains but diagnostic tests had found nothing. I called 911, and the dispatcher coached me through CPR to try and resuscitate him. With complete helplessness and despair, I watched the love of my life take his last breath and a tear roll from his eyes. The fire department arrived, and they tried to revive him, but I knew he might not be coming back when he left the house on the stretcher.

The doctor came out solemnly at the hospital and told me my husband of 4 ½ years was gone. I didn't know what to think, but I broke down in tears immediately. By the time I arrived home, many family and friends were there. I broke down again in my mother's arms. Mom had come to stay with our baby, who was only nine months at the time. God gave me so much strength to keep going. That same day, I had to process payroll for workers at the cleaners. Amazingly, I slept soundly that night and all the others. There was a scripture that comforted me…

> *"The Lord himself goes before you and will be with you;*
> *he will never leave you nor forsake you.*
> *Do not be afraid; do not be discouraged"*
>   (Deuteronomy 31:8).

A calmness overtook my body that I still can't quite explain. I never lost a night of sleep or had a feeling of helplessness or depression. The Lord started to reveal all of the amazing events and memories Horace and I had shared. That continued to put a smile on my face. He also reminded me that I had experienced having a soulmate in my life. Some people never experience that feeling.

The Lord left me with a daughter that continued to grow into a spitting image of her dad. Many people thought something was wrong because I wasn't breaking down, but I didn't, because I believed in God's plan. I looked for everything that the Lord had done versus what happened. That lead to my overcoming one of the most devastating times and events in my entire life.

In 2012, I remarried a wonderful man named Antonious Hammond. I never thought I would find love again, but I did and Antonious is a wonderful husband and amazing father to Haley. Haley recently graduated Magna Cum Laude from the University of Kentucky and is preparing to enter medical school. I have a wonderful career as the CEO of one of the largest nonprofits in the St. Louis Metro area, Challenge Unlimited, Inc., creating pathways to independence for persons with disabilities.

Through an unimaginable event and the trials of becoming a widow, single mother, and sole breadwinner overnight at the age of 32, the Lord made me stronger. Romans 5:3-5 shows us that suffering produces character and perseverance. I had to lean into God's plan for my life which required complete dependence upon His direction, purpose, fulfillment, and strength to know that I am an Overcomer.

Thank you to my village that was also part of God's plan — My mother, Verna Martin; brother, Mark Martin; family friend, William Powell; and babysitter, Verna Waters.

A tireless activist for individuals with disabilities, Charlotte Hammond, is making her mark as President and CEO of Challenge Unlimited, Inc. in Alton, IL. For more than 50 years, they have been committed to serving individuals with disabilities. Charlotte was tapped to lead the organization in 2006, after more than 20 years in corporate finance, accounting and operations management.

Under Charlotte's tutelage, the organization has received a significant number of government contracts allowing them to deliver a diverse, job-ready workforce to multiple private businesses partners across the country. The organization has also received numerous local, regional and national awards, including the 2022 MLK Award Recipient, Arcus Award for Achievement in Economic Inclusion, and the FOCUS St. Louis What's Right with the Region Award.

Charlotte is a frequent conference speaker and local media guest, and currently or has previously served on the board of directors/committees of organizations, including Chair, National Council of SourceAmerica Employers; Board Member, SourceAmerica; Commission Member, Missouri Botanical Garden; Past Board Member, ACCSES – the Voice of Disability Service Providers; Board Member, Greater St. Louis, Inc.; and Past Vice Chair, Illinois Association of Rehabilitation Facilities.

Charlotte is a wife and mother of two adult children. She lives in the St. Louis area and loves competitive professional tennis and enjoys traveling and exploring new eatery venues.

www.linkedin.com/in/charlotte-hammond-41994625

Sheena Williams

Changing the Narrative

Here it is: I'm eighteen years old, just graduated from high school, and have no clue what the next chapter is for me. All my friends are excited about going off to college. We are spending our last summer together before everyone leaves for different parts of the world. That is everyone excluding me. "Why don't I have a plan?" you may ask. Growing up, I always put school first. I had a routine; I would come home from school and work on my homework before doing anything else. I was not told to do this, it's just something I did, and it helped me stay on track while things were still "fresh in my mind.

For the most part, I had decent grades in school, not straight A's but close to it. I had family, aunts, and older cousins that went to college and received degrees, but when it came to me, it was something that never was discussed, my plans or future. My mom attended college for a short time after giving birth to me and even went away to Mississippi with me in tow; however, she and I never sat down during my senior year in high school to talk about life after.

I became very independent early in high school. Once I turned sixteen, I got my first job and took care of my necessities the remainder of my time in school. I wasn't told I needed to do this; it was just something I wanted to do. I wanted to take some of the burdens off my parents as I had a younger brother in middle school and a sister 14 years younger than me. I liked getting a job, buying my clothes and shoes, and being responsible for my school activities were helping out my parents. I remember setting up and taking my ACT twice without the help of anyone, just in case I was planning on attending college. I took it the first time my junior year to see how I would do and did just ok. So, I got a book to help me practice and retook it my senior year, doing much better. I was so excited, and then nothing. It was just not important in my home, or was I not important?

I got my high school diploma, and I guess that was good enough. I wondered if my family didn't think I was smart enough for college or not interested. I wasn't sure what to feel or think. I ended up applying with a friend to Harris Stowe State College. We both got in and were so excited about starting college together, especially since everyone else was leaving us and going away.

What was I thinking? I'm weaning life at this point. I'm a college student and have no clue or direction on what I'm doing. Maybe my parents knew something I didn't know about myself. School became less important and no one was "checking in" on me, so I dropped out. I was working job to job, hanging out, mixing in with people who didn't mean me any good, and trying to figure out life. For nearly six years, I lived a free-spirited life. I had no drive or ambition, just living day to day. Some days were great, and I enjoyed life because I was having fun, but other days, I would sit and reflect on my life. I felt sad and depressed because I knew that I wanted more for my life deep down inside. I didn't have that push that I needed to "restart" my life.

October 2007, I gave birth to my first child, my son, Nycholas. It wasn't just me trying to care for me anymore. I had another human that I had to be responsible for. I could no longer just up and quit jobs and wean anymore. It was time to be a grown-up and be accountable. During this time, I worked for a company and got promoted to a Quality Assurance Analyst. I enjoyed what I did, I was able to keep a roof over my son's head, and for the most part, things were moving in the right direction. Almost four years later, my company downsized and laid off most of its employers. I was offered the opportunity to stay with the company, and I was grateful. However, I felt like I was settling again. I went back and forth for days and would sit and think about how my son and I deserved more. Finally, I went to my supervisor and resigned from my position. It was officially time to change the narrative in my life. I made up my mind that I had to do better, not just for myself, but also for my son. I enrolled in nursing school.

Enrolling in nursing school was one of the greatest accomplishments that happened to me. I first went to school to become a Licensed Practical Nurse (LPN) because I knew I needed to do an accelerated program to complete and get back to work. I was barely surviving off unemployment and my savings. This was one of the hardest tasks I had ever conquered. I put everyone and everything on hold and hit the books. There were many tears, much stress, and sleepless nights. I learned a lot of discipline during this time. The support I was getting from my family and friends was the push I needed. They were in my corner when I needed help with my son and whatever else I needed. I can remember crying to my mom many times about things being so hard, and she would say, "You got this."

That meant the world to me. That's what I needed to hear when I graduated from high school. I felt so accomplished once I graduated and started working my first job as a Licensed Practical Nurse.

January 2014, I had been working as an LPN for a few years now and gave birth to my second child, my son, Dylan. I was living comfortably during this time. My career was going well, but my personal life and relationship with my son's father were not. I felt that my boys deserved more than the relationship their father and I provided by staying together, and it wasn't fair to them. I wasn't sure just yet what our future together would be, but I knew I needed to do what was best for our family. During this time, I decided to return to school to become a Registered Nurse. Just like before, my family and friends were right there. My children's father was no longer in the home with us, and my mom did everything for my boys as my schedule was very hectic. When I wasn't at school, I was off working. This was my life for the next few years.

I am so grateful for where I am today. This year I will celebrate ten years of being a nurse. I have taken a different approach to how I parent or interact with my children than what I had known. I try my best to ask my children what they did in school or how their day was going. We are already sitting down having small talks about college, or the next steps after graduating high school. I'm not sure what the future holds for them, but I want to be open and available to whatever they decide.

Sheena Nicole Williams was born in St Louis, Missouri, the oldest of three children.

After a career as a Quality Assurance Analyst, she obtained her Nursing Degree at Jefferson College in Missouri.

Sheena is the Founder and CEO of Endearment Home Health LLC and a Board-Certified Registered Nurse with ten years of experience, including specialties in gerontology, medical surgery, pediatrics, oncology, and community health and wellness.

Sheena enjoys spending time with her family. Whether it's dating with her husband, hanging with their three boys, traveling, cooking, or hosting a game night, she is all about making memories with her family and friends.

sjeffersonnrn@gmail.com
endearmenthomehealth@gmail.com
www.linkedin.com/in/sheena-williams-76023a22a/

Alesha Henley

Banishing the Myth: "I'm not good enough"

My mother taught me to work hard and do my best with everything I did. I was naive enough to believe working hard would be sufficient to succeed in my career. It took me a while to realize there's so much more to it than that.

You aren't going to believe it, but the story goes like this:

Once upon a time, there was a young enthusiastic marketing professional (that's me y'all). I didn't know that corporate America was all about who you know rather what you know. Indeed, I didn't understand or appreciate the importance of networking until much later in my career. Over time, I learned that my hard work merely got me more work. Every time I tried to climb the proverbial corporate ladder, there were so many barriers.

When they told me I didn't have enough education, I went back to school and received my MBA from one of the top-ranked programs in the United States, The University of Chicago Booth School of Business. I was labeled too aggressive because I had an opinion and wasn't afraid to share it. I learned to share feedback in a more palatable way with the recipient. When told I wasn't ready, I made sure I applied for roles I was 100%

qualified. I arrived in those roles 100% qualified and found my peers were only 50% qualified for their positions.

There was so much I didn't know about navigating the workplace and my career. I realized I needed a mentor, but finding one was hard. People I believed I had a real connection with didn't have time for me or couldn't provide the insight I was requesting. Maybe it was they wouldn't versus couldn't.

These barriers beat me down. Without even knowing it, I was internalizing the criticisms. I thought I had to meet all the requirements listed in the job description to apply. I didn't believe I could perform in a higher-level role because I was told, "you aren't ready." In an attempt to prove them wrong, I made lateral moves which provided more responsibility and opportunities to lead teams/committees/contractors to gain management experience. Again, I got more work, not the promotion that I desperately sought. There were few, if any, people that looked like me in positions of authority. Although I aspired to do more, I became skeptical if I truly could climb any higher than the manager level.

In June 2016, I joined a startup company as a Marketing Director. I remember it like it was yesterday. I was ready to prove all of the naysayers wrong, and I was prepared and deserved to be a Director! The truth was, I ended up being a glorified sales support person. They were not interested in marketing best practices or developing strategic approaches to reaching target audiences. They wanted someone to do what the salespeople couldn't or didn't want to. Doubt overwhelmed me, and I wondered, "Did I get the job because that is all they saw in me? Is that all I deserved? Was my work not as good as I thought?"

"Shake it off. It is not you, it's them!" is what I told myself aloud, but deep down, I wondered.

I now had corporate friends and developed a professional network that poured into me and assured me that I was good enough. I began to believe in myself and understand I could do better and deserve better.

I found an actual Marketing Director role where I established the marketing function, built a team, designed a strategy, and successfully executed the strategic plan. I was promoted to Vice President of Marketing in 12 months. My work and I were finally being noticed and rewarded. This opportunity was provided by a strong, confident African American woman who wasn't afraid to have more than one strong woman at the table. After 25 years, I finally found a mentor and ultimately a sponsor! The proverbial phrase "when life gives you lemons, make lemonade" could not have been truer in my case.

My challenges have made me committed to creating a smoother road for those that look like me or face similar struggles! I never want aspiring women or African-Americans to feel like they are not good enough.

We all have value and bring essential experiences to the table. My responsibility is to nurture the next generation, build their confidence, and help them reach goals they can't even imagine. No one gets through life without help. Most people only want a hand-up, not necessarily a handout. That is all I ever expected.

I found my path, and today the myth that I'm not good enough is debunked. I know that I'm good enough. I sit in decision-making seats that influence how the next generation of people, who look like me, is accepted, treated, and succeed in the workplace. I am where I am supposed to be, doing what I'm supposed to be doing — my small part to make the world a better place to live, work, and prosper for everyone.

I have a successful corporate and entrepreneurial career. I serve as the Senior Managing Director of the Center of Creative Arts (COCA), a non-profit arts organization that engages underserved communities in performing arts. I am also the Founder and CEO of a marketing consulting firm, a Dose of Insight, that helps professional service business owners build their brand awareness to reach and convert clients, thereby generating more revenue and growing their business.

Today, I have roles that I love. One allows me to use my professional skills to make a difference in the lives of others AND to put the icing on the cake, I own a business that helps small businesses compete and grow. I stand on the shoulders of those who came before me and fought for my seat at the table. I must stand in the gap for those who come after me. My shoulders are broad and strong to hold others up because "we are all good enough!"

Alesha Henley is an experienced marketing professional who has worked for highly branded companies. Today she is the Founder & CEO of a Dose of Insight, a marketing strategy and consulting firm. Alesha also serves as the Senior Managing Director for the Center of Creative Arts (COCA) in St. Louis.

Alesha is a forward-thinking leader that uses data and market trends to develop strategies that lead to profitable results. Her transformational leadership style innovates and creates change that helps grow and shape business success.

Alesha strives to make the world a better place for underserved people. She's an advocate for her community, participating in a range of civic organizations that improve the lives of others.

Alesha was born and raised in Cleveland, Ohio and lived in Chicagoland for more than 20 years. She resides in St. Louis with her husband.

www.adoseofinsight.com
www.facebook.com/DoseInsight
www.twitter.com/DoseInsight
www.linkedin.com/company/a-dose-of-insight/

Halima McWilliams

Living Up to My Name

I came into this world and was without a name for 21 days.

One of my family traditions is the East African practice of a naming ceremony. The naming ceremony announces the birth of a newborn. It introduces the child to their extended family and the larger community. Above all else, it confers on the child a name. The name given to a baby can have an enduring influence on their personality, upbringing, and ultimately their destiny.

My parents chose a name that ensured I would stand out before I could even speak a word: Halima (means gentle; pronounced Ha-LEE-mah) and Kianga (sunbeam; pronounced Key-yawn-GUH). My first and middle names are KiSwahili (Ki means "the way of"). KiSwahili is spoken by an estimated 80 million people in East and Central Africa and is one of the two official languages of the East African Community countries (Burundi, Kenya, Rwanda, South Sudan, Tanzania, and Uganda). I couldn't know how their ancestral covering and investment into my humanity, womanhood, and connection with the larger world would be the launchpad for the work that lay ahead for me and the work I do for others.

My siblings and many childhood friends also had naming ceremonies as a part of our jamaa (KiSwahili word for village) culture and upbringing. I grew up well aware of the meaning of my name and even the significance of the naming ceremony. However, as a child, I didn't always fully stand in the power of the uniqueness and purpose that my village envisioned for me.

Who wants to be a different kid, especially in elementary and middle school? Those are some brutal years. In school, people would often ask me about my name or make comments. Is it Hawaiian? Is it African? Can I call you something else? Do you have a nickname? Is your family from Africa? Hyena, Himalaya, and Hal can be added to the list of names given to me growing up.

On several occasions, I allowed or didn't push back on people shortening my name, appointing me nicknames, or even substituting my middle name with a more westernized and recognizable name to decrease the hassle and dim my unique light, just to fit in. Yep, guilty as charged. Even as a child, it was exhausting to explain my name's meaning, its origins, how I got it, or simply my existence in this world. Over time, there were a couple of things that I could count on: one, no one I'd ever run into would have my name, and secondly, I was uniquely made for a bigger purpose than just me.

In middle school, it began to crystallize for me that my name and purpose would be for the benefit of others. I attended St. Louis Cathedral Catholic school, and my 8th-grade teacher was Mrs. Wyman. As a part of our 8th-grade graduation, we passed around our memory autograph books that our friends, classmates, and teachers could sign with good wishes for the future. I will never forget Mrs. Wyman's parting insight and how looking back on it was a defining moment in my work today. Mrs. Wyman's note to me was, "You will always speak up and do what is just for others." I knew what the words meant at the time, but I didn't realize that using my voice for myself and others would lead me to my passion and purpose.

Over the past 25 years, I have worked as a human resources practitioner, specializing in employee relations, employee engagement and experience, and most notably diversity, equity, inclusion (DEI), and belonging. As a DEI consultant, I work with organizations, leaders, and employees in creating workplaces and environments that allow people to bring their most authentic and unique selves to work. I also charge and challenge organizations to talk in truth, acknowledge inequities, missteps, and exclusionary practices, and work collaboratively to create practices, policies, and systems that truly see, recognize, and actively include the whole human.

I have spoken at many events during my career, facilitated numerous workshops on inclusion, diversity, belonging, allyship, and many other topics that bring better awareness for marginalized communities and inspire better understanding in the workplace or outside of it. After many of these engagements, people will come up to me and share their experiences about not fully being seen, included, or valued. I'm always grateful and honored that they're comfortable enough to share their stories with me. I'm also saddened by how many of us share experiences of not being fully embraced, included, or valued. As I continue to talk with the participants or attendees, I typically share aspects of my becoming story and my overcoming journey. I encourage them to stand in their unique identity and never dim their light for anyone. Reminding them that they are wonderfully and beautifully made is always a highlight of my work.

My name means gentle sunbeam, and my purpose is to demonstrate the courtesy and kindness of humanity and cast a light on matters that affect our ability to experience the best of life. Once I fully accepted my assignment, it became easier to help others see themselves in their fullness and aid organizations in recognizing their blind spots and how those blind spots can unconsciously exclude marginalized ones. Advocating for others is never an easy lift, but it is necessary.

If we create spaces where everyone is celebrated, understood, and valued, we can wholeheartedly experience the best of each other. Whether I'm working for a corporate organization, serving on a board, doing my sorority work, or consulting, my ability and privilege to do this work will always run parallel to the work I continue to do on myself.

One of my favorite books is *The Four Agreements: A Practical Guide to Personal Freedom* by Don Miguel Ruiz. My mother, the sage woman that she is, recommended it to me years ago, and it has become a literary mainstay for me. The fourth agreement is Always Do Your Best. "Simply do your best, and you will avoid self-judgment, self-abuse, and regret," Ruiz states. I refer to this book and all the agreements throughout the year. I tell my friends about it and use it as a part of my values system regarding how I show up for myself and others.

Leaning into the principles of the fourth agreement helped me define my standard of excellence and how I want to reflect it. I believe when I am at my best, I can provide the appropriate guidance, allyship, and partnerships that propel strategic missions. When I am at my best, I can work to amplify the causes of those who are not valued or seen. And lastly, when I'm at my best, I can appreciate the wisdom, traditions, and legacies assigned to me from birth. These things have allowed me to overcome and become the full Halima Kianga, whose gentle light will leave a blueprint for others to claim their space, pull that chair up to the table, and use their voice and privilege for the good of others. In the words of my soror, the late politician Shirley Chisholm, "If they don't give you a seat at the table, bring a folding chair."

I invite you to pull up a chair, wear your natural hair, polish that crown, say your piece, and then be at peace. You are needed, valued, appreciated, and necessary.

Ase. (means "so it is," in Kiswahili)

Halima K. McWilliams, MS, PHR, CDP is an enthusiastic culture strategist, speaker, and passionate employee experience advocate. She leverages her knowledge and expertise of more than 25 years of experience in Diversity, Equity & Inclusion (DEI) and strategic HR to aid organizations in crafting customized, practical and realistic solutions that work.

Halima's down-to-earth, friend-next-door energy compels individuals to consider the perspectives of others, appreciate our flawed humanity and activate childlike curiosity while they learn. She engages groups from the moment she steps in front of them and leaves them with empowering tools and focused mindsets that they will use long after the learning experience is over. Halima is passionate about people, leadership accountability, and leaving positive light and love after each interaction. She is especially inspired to use her platform to educate and amplify those who are often on the margins.

Halima is a nationally certified HR & Diversity Executive. She also is a certified Enterprise Design Thinking practitioner via IBM. She holds a Bachelor of Arts in Psychology from the University of Missouri – St. Louis and a Master of Science in Human Resource Management from Capella University. Halima has worked in leadership roles in Fortune 500 organizations in various industries such as aerospace and defense, financial services, healthcare and architecture, and design.

When not speaking, leading, or training, Halima hangs out with her husband, Jason, at their home in Dallas. They love exploring new restaurants and live music concerts, especially smooth jazz and neo-soul.

www.linkedin.com/in/halimakconsults

www.youtube.com/channel/UCQrfDXIh7Ua6d8Jos4QPdWw

facebook.com/halimakconsults

www.instagram.com/halimakconsults/

Rachel R. Jackson

Go Through Your Valley

"You will not lose your mind today."

This is what I woke up and told myself every day in 2000 and for the first one year after unexpectedly losing my mother at the age of nineteen. My ability to fully comprehend how and why this was happening to me wasn't entirely possible. Deeply hurt and overwhelmed with feeling abandoned by her passing, I felt all I had was my mind left. If I could keep my mind, I would make it through this.

"You can't die here."

This is what I told myself from 2014 to 2016 after filing for divorce, and my ex-husband abruptly stopped fulfilling his financial obligations and becoming someone I never knew. The fear and frustration that consumed me each day made me feel that I had come to the end of my road. My body started physically giving out on me. I endured two emergency surgeries struggled with exhaustion and fatigue for 2 years. I was also enrolled in a master's program for Professional Counseling while working full-time.

A very dark valley lay between where I was then and now. It rained in that valley every day. I just showed up every day as a mother, sister, friend, and business owner expected to perform each role, but I didn't have the strength. I just walked through the valley — piece by piece. I had to deal with it all.

Deep down, I just wanted God to fix it all. I was exhausted. God never spoke a word, and I barely could see Him moving on my behalf, yet I knew He was there. He was with me. I made bad choices and a few mistakes. Yes, it made some things worse, but it was my valley. This journey felt personal, and it was truly between God and me. While others found it easy to offer opinions or judge the pieces they could see, I just wanted support through what they couldn't see.

Everything around me was growing, yet I felt like I would die trying to carry three children as their provider, mother, and the weight the community had now placed on my shoulder by declaring me a "Woman of Worth." Yet, this battle left me feeling unworthy.

Was my mother's death the punishment for the disobedience of my youth? Was the financial drought the result of my filing for divorce?

"GIRL, what have you done? How did you allow yourself to get here?"

I was in more than a battle for peace of mind, and I was in a fight for my life. I had to finish everything I had started. I knew on the other side was everything I had ever prayed for.

I refused to die, and my mind became my greatest weapon.

Over the years, I've leaned into the promises of God more than I ever had in my life. It was His word that allowed me to have hope. I stood firm on knowing that if I survived that, surely, I would survive this. I had to embrace the reality I was walking through my life valley. And even though I felt like I could die at times, my soul would remind me daily of Psalm 23, "The Lord is my shepherd; I shall not want. He maketh me to lie down in green pastures: he leadeth me beside the still waters. He restoreth my soul: he leadeth me in the paths of righteousness for his name's sake. Yea, though I walk through the valley of the shadow of death, I will fear no evil: for thou art with me; thy rod and thy staff they comfort me. Thou preparest a table before me in the presence of mine enemies: thou anoints my head with oil; my cup runneth over. Surely goodness and mercy shall follow me all the days of my life."

This was my new normal. I was walking in the valley of the shadow of death. Being afraid and worrying would have been easy. I chose to fear no evil each day and allow God to comfort me. Make no mistake, I am no saint, but I am faithful to my relationship with God. He didn't need me perfect. He needed me to show up each day willing.

I knew God was with me. His goodness and mercy were following me. That became my daily reminder. I had no reason to fear anything or anyone because God was with me.

Each day, His presence was felt.

I felt it when starting a nonprofit, Project Compassion, NFP, with a heart full of gratitude and compassion at the age of 25, in the small victories in court, and when my health was restored. I felt it when finishing with a 4.0 GPA and carrying the division banner on graduation day with a Master's in Professional Counseling. His presence gave me the strength to raise my children, the ability to laugh amid the sadness, and the calls for positions and roles I never applied for. It was also in the growth of my businesses, opening my heart to love and being loved again. It was feeling worthy and knowing that I was worth everything good that came for and to me.

I realized I hadn't lost anything that I had only grown. I had been reminded that not only was God FOR me, HE was WITH me.

The seasons I felt made to destroy me taught me how to praise God in true spirit and truth.

In the Bible, the story of Job has inspired many. I felt like Job some days. While having my Job moment, I realized it wasn't His patience that I needed. It was His praise. In Job:1, after Job found out he lost all of His children, He tore His clothes, shaved His head, and cried out in verse 21 and said, "Naked came I out of my mother's womb, and naked shall I return thither: the Lord gave, and the Lord hath taken away; blessed be the name of the Lord." "God giveth, and God takes away, blessed be the name of the Lord."

It was the "blessed be the name of the Lord" that moved me. In his greatest moment of loss, pain, sadness, and suffering, Job had praise!! That's what I wanted. I wanted to look beyond all that I had lost and praise God for "giving" me anything at all. A phenomenon mother who loved God had raised us with a strength and wisdom like no other woman I've ever met in my life. I wanted to praise God for giving me a family for 12 years. I wanted to praise God for giving me three beautiful, funny, and healthy children to love. I wanted to praise God for my health and strength. I had to shift my mindset from loss to gratitude. I had to change my perspective. It wasn't about what I didn't have. It was about everything I did have and everything I could gain again.

During my Job moments, I kept reminding myself that my prayers are necessary, but my praise is crucial. I started each day with praise instead of a prayer. I started celebrating small victories, and suddenly I realized I was winning every day. It was all in the perspective which increased my praise. I also had to forgive. Forgiveness was the key that unlocked the door. I first forgave myself. I restored myself to the standard of excellence I was formed to be. I reminded myself that I was truly fearfully and wonderfully made, and no one can ever alter that image of me because it was never theirs to create. I then forgave those that had intentionally or unintentionally hurt and betrayed me. I freed them and myself. I restored relationships with those who truly valued me, and I felt we could journey in true love. I also released those that I knew were not for me. That included friends with a history so long and beautiful. That also included family. It's something about surviving the people and things meant to kill you that leaves you stronger and wiser. You tend to be braver!

I'll leave you with this. The mountain that won't move, the sea that won't part and the valley that appears to be never-ending is a part of the process. Don't die trying to climb. Don't drown trying to swim and whatever you do, don't stop. Go through your valley.

My daily scripture reminder is 2 Corinthians 4:8:

"We are pressed on every side, but not crushed; we are perplexed, but not in despair; persecuted, but not abandoned, struck down, but not destroyed."

Rachel R. Jackson founded Project Compassion, NFP (PC-NFP) when she was 25 years old. Since 2005, PC-NFP has assisted more than 80,000 homeless, disadvantaged, and low-income men, women, and children with food, shelter, seasonal supplies, hygiene items, life skills workshops, and vocational training.

Rachel is a motivational and inspirational speaker that has shared her inspiring story of "living with a Brave Heart" and empowered many more to do the same.

Rachel launched the first *self-esteem and self-worth* program called Empower-Me in St. Clair County, IL working with school districts to inspire youth and girls by building beauty from the inside first, building character, and continuing education. Rachel is the host of the Girlz On Purpose Tour.

Rachel holds a B.S in Business Administration and M.A in Professional Counseling; Certified Master Trainer in Life Skills, and self-esteem. Rachel is a Certified Civil and Divorce Mediator.

Rachel has received local and national awards for her work, including the...

- BASIC Citizen of Character Award
- 2014 L'Oreal Paris Woman of Worth

- Barack Obama Silver Presidential Award for her community service
- Daily Point of Light Award
- Lindenwood University Outstanding Alum Award
- Top Ladies of Distinction "Extraordinary Women"
- Delta Economic Development Corp Award "Heroes Among Us"
- TOCO "Making a Difference" Award

In 2011, Rachel opened the Compassionate Resource Center in Belleville, IL and received a proclamation from the Mayor of Belleville, IL, declaring October 29th "Compassion Day" in Belleville in 2014.

Rachel's mission has received media attention including the...

- Tyra Banks Show: received the *Secret Deodorant Strong Enough for a Woman Award*.
- ABC Radio: The Powerful Difference Award by Pine-Sol
- Ebony Magazine: featured June 2008, December 2014
- Additional Magazine Exposure: MORE, Oprah (O), Glamour, Gazelle, and Southern Living
- Black Professional Women (2011 & 2016) honored as a Racial Harmony Phenomenal Woman
- United Way honoree at the 2013 *Volunteer Honors Banquet*

www.facebook.com/IamRachelRenata

www.instagram.com/iamrachelrenata

www.linkedin.com/in/rachel-renata-530a0612/

www.rachelrenata.com

www.projectcompassionnfp.org

Lashanda Barnes

Overcoming Silence: Speaking My Power

Babies learn language by sight and sound. Ma Ma, Da Da, Ba Ba and NO! Nothing more than simple babbling except the word NO! Babies typically enunciate NO in its full entirety as a complete word that is belted out with confidence and conviction with the deliberate intention of rejecting or stopping something undesired. What happens to our no, our voice, our power as we grow older? What becomes of the undesirables in our lives if we lose it? What follows is a reflection on the evolution of my no, my voice, my power.

Around age seven or eight I spent the night at a relative's house. I woke up in the middle of the night to use the bathroom. When I came out of the bathroom, "Come in here, you can sleep in this bed," a male voice said. So, I did. I hopped in bed and got under the covers. I laid down on my side. HE spooned me from the back. Then slid my panties down. I pulled them back up. HE slid them down again. This sequence repeated. Then I felt something between my legs. I didn't know what. It wasn't cloth, it felt fleshy. It wasn't a hand. There were no words spoken. There were thoughts in my head, a queasy feeling in my stomach, and my heartbeat was loud and rapid. All of which I now understand to have been physiological and psychological bells and whistles that indicated that this should not have been happening. I wanted to yell NO! But pulling my panties back up didn't help. I didn't want to disrespect an adult. Without my NO, I was respectfully powerless.

About a year later, HE visited my family home. I was in a bedroom watching TV. HE came in. I sat up on the side of the bed. My feet dangled. He told me to scratch his back. I did. He raised his shirt so that I could scratch his bare back. His skin peeled and got under my fingernails. Gross. I stopped. He started kissing me gently on my neck then my stomach lowering his head before starting to tug on my shorts to pull them down. I pushed his head away. No words were spoken. There were words of protest in my head, but my mouth was silent. He stopped and looked in my eyes not with intimidation but with surprise. He was kissing my stomach again. NO, STOP! I said firmly without yelling. At the same time, I pushed him with as much force as a little girl can push a grown man. "You pushed me?" he asked rhetorically as if trying to solve a riddle. He stopped and never tried to touch me again. I used my voice, my NO, my power to reject/stop the undesired.

About ten years later, I had spent a beautiful early summer day in the park with my favorite male cousin, and some friends. The outing was everything I loved: fresh air, sunshine, family, R&B, and awesome food. My son's father, Easy (E), inserted himself into my plans for the day. Technically, he was still my boyfriend but I checked out of the relationship during my pregnancy the night he got drunk and tried to choke me in his parent's laundry room. He promised to never put his hands on me or drink around me again. At this point, I was just doing what I thought a mother should do, stay with their child's father.

By dusk, Easy was up dancing and cracking jokes, super social… Drunk. Meet Eight Ball Easy (EBE). Eight Ball is the nickname for 40-ounce single containers of beer that had been outlawed in our state. Apparently drinking the equivalent of 3 1/4 beers in one sitting makes consumers act a fool. Against my wishes, EBE drove us to my cousin's house for the afterparty, where he drank more.

We left my cousin's at about 10. "Where are you going? You guys are going home with me." "NEGATIVE," I said in my head. My mouth said, "I am tired. I want to go home and get our son to bed." No response. I woke up in his mother's driveway. She was sitting on the porch. "I was hotter than fish grease," as my friend's mom would say. "Take us home. I want to go home." Slam. He gets out of the car. I don't move. He goes to the porch and stares in the direction of the car. I don't move. "Lashanda get out the car so that I can turn my alarm on." Seriously? His family is in this car and his priority is to turn the alarm on to protect the car? I felt a strong tug as he pulled me from the car to the middle of the yard. Just take us home! "Shut up before my neighbors hear you!" "I don't give a … BAM!" The sound of his right fist slamming full force into my left jaw. This was not a love tap and he didn't hit like a girl. He hit like a Ninja, as if in a man-on-man brawl. I had no time to contemplate the pain or shock of being struck by a man for the first time. Only time to contemplate avoid getting hit twice. Instinctively, I fell out as if he had knocked me off my feet. Like a wrestler but more realistic. His mother jumped up and yelled, "If y'all got to fight, y'all don't need to be together!" Seriously? I'm lying in the middle of her yard because her son tried to knock the sense out of my head. What fight? He punched me; I fell out. PERIOD.

He helped me up. Chivalry? "I'll take her home," he claimed. "Take her straight home," she replied. I remembered those public service announcements that warn not to leave with the stranger. Stalling, I used his parents' house phone to call my cousin. "Come get me." CLICK. That's all I said. He lived 10 minutes away. That was ten minutes too far because without my consent his mother made a deal with the devil to take me home. The next several hours were as bizarre as they were terrifying. He drove to every dark nook and cranny in St. Louis County.

"If I can't have you, no one will," and "I will kill you then, kill myself," He threatened repeatedly. "Give me another chance." He was out of his head. Multiple times he parked and uncontrollably banged his head against the windshield or the steering wheel. I prayed that he would knock himself out, but he didn't.

He drove to his friend house and left us in the car. I opened the door and took off running! He followed but couldn't catch me. Around the corner, I hid behind the dumpster of an old laundromat. Now I'm terrified of the darkness. Across the street was a brightly lit wing house full of customers. I darted across the street and swung the door open. Everyone turned around, and all eyes were on me. I sighed in relief. I was safe. I recognized a classmate and her boyfriend. Suddenly embarrassment and shame overwhelmed me. Then everyone's eyes shifted to the door behind me. I waited for someone to help or to ask, "Are you alright?" No one did. Defeated. I said nothing. He yanked my arm, I didn't protest. Back in the car, I said, "E, I can't live like this." "I promise to stop drinking," he responded. This is your last chance, I promised. "Lashanda, don't lie to me." E take us home. He did.

I unlocked the front door and placed my son's car seat inside the house. With my back to the door, I said, "Now get the "F" off my porch before I wake my brother." His expression was unmistakable, he wanted to kill me. I had no idea where my brother was but I knew E didn't want to SEE him. Defeated, he left. It was 5 a.m., my cousin and brother had been out all night looking for me. "Did he hit you?" my brother asked. I will blow his house up. Please don't. You will never see me with him again. He hasn't.

Nine months later EBE broke into my cousin's house where I was babysitting. I heard the commotion. I locked the bedroom door where I was hiding with our son and my cousin's daughter. Boom! Easy entered the room and put a gun to the right of my head. "If I can't have you, then no one will have you. I'm going to kill you then kill myself." I decided that I'd rather be dead than not really be living. "You'll have to kill me." He didn't. He left.

Proverbs 18:21 states that the tongue has the power of life and death. I used the power in my tongue to stop a predator and to save my life. Today I am living my best life whole, happy, healthy, and free and you can do the same.

Lashanda Barnes grew up in Wellston, in St. Louis County Missouri, the youngest of seven siblings. She has a BA in Organizational Studies and a Masters of Management from Fontbonne University, in Missouri, and is Vice President at a major global financial services firm as an exemplary risk mitigator. Public speaking and writing are her superpowers.

Lashanda is a proud member of St. Louis Alumnae Chapter of Delta Sigma Theta Sorority Incorporated; a member of the St. Louis Children's Hospital Board of Trustees; Co-Chair of the St. Louis Regional Business Council Young Professionals Steering Committee and Network; and a Social Ventures Partners board member.

The St. Louis American Newspaper has honored her with their Young Leader award. The St. Louis Business Journal honored her with their Diverse Leader award.

Her personal Mission Statement, "To strive for excellence, listen with the intent to understand, give more than I take, and respect all persons." She is a loving mother to her adult son and nana to his amazing children. She enjoys hosting family gatherings, playing music, dancing, traveling, brunching, and learning golf.

www.facebook.com/profile.php?id=100073812927985
www.linkedin.com/in/lashanda-barnes-78b91b33

Taraya J. Shirdan

Now…It's On Me

It was an ordinary hot August day. Through an open window in our living room, I could hear the kids playing outside; as I turn, my mother says, "Shouldn't you be getting ready to head back to school?" I glanced at her and my grandmother with a matter-of-fact look and said," Oh, I didn't tell you?... I'm not going back."

They were both stunned. My mother, practically stuttering, asked, "Well, well...what...what are you going to do?" I explained that I would take some classes at the local university and figure it out. At this point, my mother's stuttering was completely cured when she emphatically stated, "'Well, I paid for you to go to Howard… Now, it's on you!"

"Now it's on me"……. I decided to leave Howard University because I knew that as a liberal arts major, with no clear career path in mind. I was left to the mercy of parties, fraternity events, and any other reason not to go to class. I even failed choir. I had no idea it counted toward my GPA. To this very day, I still don't understand how a teenager at the tender age of 17 or 18 could know what they wanted to do for the rest of their life. I sure didn't. I was, however, smart enough to know that I wasn't going to figure it out at the parties. So, when I left, I left for good.

I had to figure out what I wanted to do, how to make it happen, and how to pay for it. …Now it's really on me. After taking some classes and researching the health care field, I knew I wanted to become a physical therapist. There were only two physical therapy programs in Philadelphia at that time.

Pre-requisite courses were the most challenging courses for me, primarily sciences. Approximately 1500-plus students apply to each program every year, with a maximum capacity of only 50 students. Not to mention the programs were costly. It was an uphill journey with the promise of securing a good-paying job wherever I wanted. I could work in a hospital, work with professional athletes, teach at a university, become a researcher, or even own private practice. I knew I was on the right path. I completed the pre-requisite courses by day and worked at a department store by night. The program requirements also included volunteering in a physical therapy facility and submitting a letter of recommendation from a physical therapist.

Sadly, cleaning the whirlpool tubs and re-stocking patient towels were my only responsibilities as a volunteer in the physical therapy department at the hospital. I wanted more exposure but was happy to do anything the supervising therapist told me to do. I observed as much as possible while changing linens near the patients. I was on time, all the time, never late, never absent for six months. The day came when I would request my letter of recommendation.

I stood at her desk in her office. The supervising physical therapist sat in her swivel chair, looked me in the eye, and preceded to tell me she would *not* write my letter. She started with, "As you know, physical therapy is a very competitive field, and we are *very particular* about who we want in our profession. "Further, I don't feel I know you well enough."

Six months on my knees cleaning nasty whirlpool tubs for this? I knew how the world worked, but somehow, I didn't see this one coming; then, it hit me like a bat upside my head. Her white plainness and unattractiveness suddenly stood out to my eye. The condescending tone of her voice was loud to my ear, and racism painfully pierced my heart. Fortunately, my pride was still in control because I refused to let her see the devastation I felt. My eyes swelled with tears, but I would not let them fall before I left her.

I was a threat? My blackness was a threat. I told myself …one day… I will be back for your job, Honey!

I submitted my applications to the programs without a letter of recommendation from a therapist. However, the wait was like most college admission decisions; this one weighed heavy on my mind and spirit. I had come too far from those parties on the hill. I was two years in Chemistry, Physics, Biology, and cleaning whirlpool tubs. I didn't have a plan B, but I had faith in myself. After all, now it was on me, so I had to.

The phrase, "We are very particular about who we want in our profession," played over and over in my head. I was still hopeful, but I was not accepted to either program. I tried to justify my sadness and disappointment. "Well, the programs only had 50 slots, so it was a long shot anyway." What now??? Now it's on me, and it's not like me to quit. I had to try again, but somebody had to tell me what I needed to do the next time differently! This was not tenacity; this was common sense.

The very next week, I was on the phone. I decided that Jefferson University was a better fit than the other program; it was new and much more expensive. I called, and the admission director was on a call. I called again, and the admission director was in a meeting or out of the office. I called again; the admission director was on vacation. I called again and again, until he finally took the call from this persistent Black girl. I asked him to please tell me what I need to do to enhance my chances the next time. He pulled up my application and my records.

"Miss Johnson," he said, "Your grades aren't too bad. I tell you what… take Anatomy and Physiology I and II, then call me back. I can't guarantee you anything, but take those courses and send me your grades." It took a few extra moments to process what the admission director said.

I had just been given a second chance.

In those days, there was no internet, so I searched the local telephone directory to find colleges and universities that offered Anatomy and Physiology I and II. It was June by this time, and the semester for the physical therapy program was due to start in September. Most schools did not offer the courses. By the grace of God, I found two colleges at opposite ends of the city that offered them. Unfortunately, they were scheduled at the same time. The community college was in the city, and the Catholic College was in the suburbs. Anatomy and Physiology II was in the morning, and Anatomy/Physiology I was in the evening. I had to call my grandmother and ask her for the money to pay tuition. She always came through for me. Now, I had to ask the department store where I was employed to move my weekday hours to weekends only. This was all a long shot. If the stars needed to be moved and aligned, I had to ask the powers to be; because now it was on me.

I took the courses, worked on weekends, and studied whenever I could. Summer school classes are intense because they cram a typical course semester into a few weeks. I had to get A's, or my chances to reverse the admission decision would be slim. I managed to get a GPA of 92. Who knew that the Catholic college had a different grading scale? Their grading scale was different than the other schools', and I had no idea. A grade of 93+ was the equivalent of an A. I received a 92. Are you kidding me??? There she was again in my head. "We are very particular about who we want in our profession," and I got a B.

I sent my grades to the director of admissions and waited with bated breath. In late August, another letter arrived at my mother's house from the Department of Admissions. This time it felt different than when the first rejection letters came. I put so much effort, energy, and hope into this. I didn't want all that to be taken away by a simple glance at a piece of paper. I looked at the sealed envelope for a couple of days then finally opened it.

One white woman and two predominately white schools told me no, but I wouldn't let that end my story. I got admitted that September. I worked twice as hard to stay in. I graduated and passed the state boards. I never did go back to get her job. However, I started my private practice serving thousands of inner-city Black children in Philadelphia. And… I employ several physical therapists that look just like her, but they are treated equitably with dignity and respect.

"You can do anything you want to do. Life is a gift, so be thankful, be thoughtful, and make the most of it. And above all, make a difference."

Taraya Shirdan, founder and president of Sunshine Therapy Club, Inc., has dedicated her life to making a difference.

She earned a Bachelor's degree in Physical Therapy from Thomas Jefferson University's College of Allied Health Sciences in Philadelphia, PA. She subsequently received a Master's degree in Early Childhood Education and Child Development from the University of Pennsylvania.

Sunshine Therapy Club was established in 1999, with a mission to empower families so that they can empower their children, Sunshine Therapy Club provides physical therapy, occupational therapy, speech therapy, special instruction, nutrition, and social work services to hundreds of children and families in the Philadelphia area. Since its inception, it has provided services to thousands of children.

Today, Taraya continues to coach business owners, managers, and others in leadership roles while building her coaching business.

www.sunshinetherapyclub.com
www.facebook.com/taraya.shirdan.9
www.instagram.com/tarayashirdan/
tarayashirdancoaching@gmail.com
tj.shirdan@sunshinetherapyclub.com

Alana Pease

Any Given Sunday

5-6, 5-6-7-8…resounded St. Louis' distinguished choreographer Ray Parks, directing over 60 dancers to assemble and launch into a high-energy performance quickly. For three straight hours on a Saturday night, he demanded straight lines, high kicks, accentuated moves, attitude, and a flawless routine in unison.

With great prowess, the competition was fierce. It was difficult to hide among so many talented dancers if you didn't bring your A-game. Knowing I lacked some technical skills, compared to others who had been classically trained, I was determined to exceed his expectations and strived to master the performances. I had to prove my worth and that I deserved to be there. Even more so, I wanted to be someday chosen to take a position on the front row, which was every dancer's pinnacle achievement.

"One-mo-again," he'd shout, in his own humorous but serious way, instructing one more run-through. We'd pretend not to glance at the clock and hold back our frustration because rehearsal should have ended 30 minutes ago. Doesn't he realize we want to hit the party scene or even get our beauty rest before tomorrow's game? Hoping to earn his sympathy while at a near breaking point, we'd inexplicably deliver again and again.

It's showtime! Sunday was game day, and there I was performing before 40,000 fans at Busch Stadium as a professional NFL cheerleader for the St. Louis Cardinals. This was my world with the St. Louis Professional Cheerleaders and Dancers Association for the next eight years. We represented all St. Louis' professional sports teams, including Steamers and Ambush soccer teams, and promotional appearances for Blues hockey. We were everywhere: on posters, in parades, traveling, media blitzes, and corporate events. The experience was amazing, notwithstanding certain pressures and demands of the industry.

Immediately following high school, at age 17, I joined hundreds of young women and auditioned for one of few open positions. Despite it being the most grueling audition, I survived two days of intense competition and won over the judges. I recall breathing a sigh of relief watching several girls walk away in tears with disappointment. I was completely surprised; I made a strong impression and was selected.

At that moment, I decided to delay my college plans to 'go pro.' Before sharing the excitement with my parents, I made it sound logical. Was I making a mistake? Deciding not to follow my classmates on the traditional path to higher learning, I admittedly had second thoughts. Even more so, 'professional cheerleading' was not a career goal discussed with my guidance counselor, nor imagined in a dream. Settling into the reality of the moment, I enjoyed the thought of creating my path and taking a chance. Fortunately, my parents gave me the freedom to think independently and work towards what made me happy — as long as I had a plan.

I was voted "most likely to succeed" throughout my early school years; I thought it was a meager and ambiguous award. It didn't have the clout or feel as rewarding as earning the highest academic achievement or superlative awards presented to my peers. Not until much later in life did I understand its significance. It was a prophecy by teachers who could envision my future when I couldn't. The votes of confidence and encouragement were small crumbs that became reminders of my potential and responsibility to live up to its reverence.

But what glitters isn't always gold, nor was I satisfied with just being a local celebrity. Although juggling a demanding schedule was crazy and exciting, I didn't feel a total sense of accomplishment. Within seven years, I expedited my career plan. I simultaneously worked towards a Bachelor's degree in Marketing, an MBA, and a full-time corporate career. And, if that weren't enough, I married my college sweetheart. Over the years, I became empowered and headstrong, reevaluating and leveraging many opportunities.

While committed to dancing, I gained an abundance of competencies that gave me an advantage in navigating my professional career. Yet, there were formidable lessons along the way. There's an aspect of the entertainment industry that is frequently overlooked: self-doubt and insecurity. Continuous judging was unhealthy, leaving many young women to feel broken and unworthy with a lingering what-if. A lesson I've learned is 'what gets you there doesn't keep you there,' so negativity becomes self-inflicted.

Auditioning as a dancer was no different than applying for colleges or corporate jobs. They all have a common thread — the selection process.

I can attest that these experiences have led to inadequacy and lowered self-esteem, while transparency and honest feedback is seldom offered. Open dialogue could potentially minimize the thought of subjective influences prompted by sexism, racism, or biases. Hearing no from judges or employers inspired me to support women who were left second-guessing themselves and wondering, "why not me?"

Reflecting back, I was young and naive. I sought assimilation to cope or blend in and gain acceptance. As one of the youngest on the team, my limited exposure to worldly encounters and my slender figure played a part in my desire for a curvier body type. Never before had I lacked confidence. However, I wasn't prepared for the judgment and scrutiny it took to be both glamorous and talented without comparing myself. The racial makeup of the dance team skewed predominantly white, while minorities represented less than 10%. This meant chances were slim for making it to the front row as it was generally reserved for only one minority at a time. This wasn't a hard rule, but it was a common practice. Little did I know this was how the world limited the presence and exposure of black women. Ill-equipped without long blonde hair or the sex appeal of my dance counterparts, I had to figure out a formula to succeed in this environment. So, I changed my look, lengthened my hair, and even modified my food intake to meet each week's weight requirement. Fortunately, this was short-lived as my girlfriends were the positive influences and images of beautiful black women that encouraged me to reclaim my A-game and focus on promoting my best assets. I began studying the art of showmanship and discovered multiple ways to increase my visibility, and soon I attracted opportunities made just for me.

An insightful quote from world-renowned motivational speaker Les Brown helped me to live by the guiding principle: *"It is better to be prepared and not have an opportunity than to have an opportunity and not be prepared."*

Beyond the game and performances, I have become an effective communicator. Networking with sponsors and talking to the public and media became a training ground to practice public speaking. Although I never found the appetite to immerse myself in professional sports, these experiences taught me how to shift the conversations away from sports toward a more balanced topic. Honing this skill changed my career trajectory, created broader circles, and increased my ability to network in male-dominated circles comfortably. I attribute my professionalism and polished soft skills to these encounters.

While auditions were held each year with no guarantee of being invited back to the team, competing for most of my life made interviewing for the workforce less intimidating. When preparing for job interviews, I understood the importance of 1) preparation, 2) presentation, and 3) presence. These characteristics led me to marketing careers with Coca-Cola, L'Oreal, and Nestle. Most rewarding, I became an entrepreneur and launched a professional development and coaching practice, HeadStrong Leader LLC, which may indicate that 'most likely to succeed' now has a special meaning. I approach my newest endeavor as an executive of a fintech start-up company with total confidence and assurance of my self-worth. This role wildly compliments my temperament for new adventures. Each progressive step has shaped me into the woman I am today.

As I matured, I found stillness. Moments of encouragement and reminders of self-worth let me know that I have broken the mold and cultivated a solid foundation. I've concluded that it's okay to borrow attributes and styles from others but don't become an imitation. I recognize some crumbs may not be intended for me and are to be examined and not consumed. These are crumbs that others have stepped on, stepped over, or possibly even spit out. I must collect only what fulfills my vision and leave the rest behind.

Permitting myself to take the road less traveled always required faith, boldness, and hustle. Even as a performer, I had to be willing to step out of line and stop focusing on the "front row" as there were other positions and opportunities within my reach. Life has taught me that if I wait in the shadows, I'll never feel the light, but the light will find me when I make my own moves.

As women, we must not passively wait in line for something better. We must not follow the crowd or only traditional paths to get ahead. We must break new ground to allow for authenticity, originality, and a new direction. It is freedom.

Alana Pease is an executive coach, speaker, and leader. She is CEO and Executive Coach of HeadStrong Leader LLC and Chief of Staff of Proforma Inc., a developing and growing new financial services startup company.

An advocate for women business leaders and young professionals, Alana coaches her clients on personal branding, team collaboration, and how to thrive in corporate cultures.

Alana received a Bachelor's degree in Marketing and MBA from Lindenwood University, and a graduate coaching certification from ICF accredited CoachU. She serves on the board of directors of Promise Community Homes.

A native of St. Louis, Alana enjoys business coaching, Zumba, and cycling with her husband, Al. Together they've raised three amazing future leaders, Bryce, Ivana, and Christian.

Headstrongleader@gmail.com
www.linkedin.com/in/alanapease/

Rev. Angela M. Tate

Overcoming My 6

I am not supposed to be here. It seems like a pretty dramatic statement, I know. It is, indeed, a true statement. I am not supposed to be "here."

Here is a place of success, security and safety, good health, healthy relationships, contentment, and ambition. Why then would I say that I am not supposed to be here? It's connected to where my life started and all that I had to overcome to get here.

The CDC and Kaiser Permanente conducted a study from 1995-1997 to examine the impact of childhood abuse and neglect and other household challenges on later-life health and well-being. It was called the Adverse Childhood Experiences Study (ACES) and consisted of 10 questions to determine how many adverse experiences or traumas individuals had been exposed to before turning 18. Trauma, by definition, results from exposure to an incident or series of events that are emotionally disturbing or life-threatening with lasting adverse effects on an individual's functioning and mental, physical, social, emotional, and spiritual well-being.

Questions from the ACES survey include:
- Before your 18th birthday, did a parent or other adult in the household often or very often swear at you, insult you, put you

down or humiliate you or act in a way that made you afraid that you might be physically hurt?
- Did a parent or other adult push, grab, slap or throw something at you? Or ever hit you so hard that you had marks or were injured?
- Did you often or very often feel that you didn't have enough to eat, had to wear dirty clothes, and had no one to protect you? Or were your parents too drunk or high to take care of you or take you to the doctor if you needed it?

Other questions gathered information about exposure to mental illness, suicide, imprisoned household members, and whether parents were separated or divorced.

Each of the 10 questions that the respondent answered yes to, counted as a point. At the end of the survey, the total number of points resulted in a score that ranged from 0 -10. With a score of 0, you had not been exposed to any adverse childhood experiences. A score of 10 means you had been exposed to all 10 before turning 18.

ACEs are common. Nearly two-thirds of adults have experienced at least one adverse childhood experience.

ACEs are detrimental. Being exposed to 1 or more ACE can cause adult onset of chronic diseases such as cancer and heart disease and contribute to mental illness, violence, and being a victim of violence.

ACEs don't occur alone. If you have one, there's an 87% chance of having two or more. Multiple ACEs are damaging and potentially deadly. The more ACEs you have, the greater the risk for long-term health challenges.

In my first year of graduate school, while I was pursuing my counseling degree, I had the opportunity to take the ACEs survey. The focus of the class I was taking was to explore those things from my past that could negatively impact my work as a counselor. Many people go into the helping field due to their own traumatic experiences; however, people must go through their healing process first. How could I ever hope to be used as an instrument in someone else's healing journey if I was still wounded myself? It was probably one of the first occasions I had to be completely honest about experiences that I had either forgotten, totally suppressed, or just passed off as part of a normal upbringing. Completing the survey, I was surprised to see that I answered yes to 6 of the ten survey statements. I was a 6.

I was surprised partly because before the survey, if someone asked about my childhood, I would say that I had a good childhood. I never considered that there was anything necessarily traumatic in my past. Sure, things weren't perfect, and there were challenges, but I never felt anything traumatic in my past. One of the first things I had to overcome was the tendency to normalize the abnormal. As I reflected on my answers to the survey, I had to acknowledge and accept that it was not normal to hide in the bathroom whenever I would feel intense emotions so that no one would see me cry. I had to acknowledge and accept that it was not normal to grow up in an environment of regular cursing, yelling, name-calling, and threatening. I had to acknowledge and accept that it was not normal having my hand held over fire on a stove as punishment for playing with matches. Overcoming the tendency to normalize the abnormal was not easy. Acknowledging and accepting these truths about my life felt like disrespect and a betrayal of my biological mother, who died 13 years earlier. What I came to understand was that I could embrace my reality and empathize with hers at the same time. I learned that I could still feel all the love and admiration that I did for her and, at the same time, admit that she was flawed. She loved me dearly and deeply, and she did the best that she could.

I then had to overcome the impact of my 6. The statistics dictate that because of my 6, I should be uneducated, unmarried, and divorced, have children by multiple men, be a victim of domestic violence, be addicted to drugs and alcohol, live a sedentary lifestyle, be underemployed, have numerous health challenges, and have my life cut short by 20 years.

These statistics dictate a very different reality than the one I am currently experiencing. The statistics dictate that I be uneducated, yet I have a master's degree, professional licensure, and plans for further education. The statistics dictate that I should have children by multiple men and be unmarried, and those children should also be uneducated. Yet, I have been married to the same man for over 20 years, and we have two young adult daughters who are both college graduates. The statistics dictate that I be underemployed. Yet, I have a fulfilling career doing what I believe I was put on this earth to do, including full-time vocational ministry as ordained clergy, serving as a college professor, and being a business owner operating my private counseling practice helping others to heal from their trauma. The statistics dictate that I live a sedentary lifestyle with multiple health challenges. Yet, I have a clean bill of health and have run 28 full marathons with aspirations to run a total of 50.

Ultimately, I had to overcome the notion that I have to be strong all the time as I deal with the challenges resulting from my 6. Resilience is a character trait long attributed to African-American women. There are worse traits to be associated with, so this is not a bad thing at face value, and I gladly list resiliency as one of the ways I would describe myself. However, this resilience and the expectation that each time I show up, I will be strong, unshakable, powerful, bold, commanding, and always put together has created a burden that often is too great to bear. Yes, I am strong, but I need space to be weak some days. I am powerful and bold, but I need space to be quiet some days. Some days I need space to be. My 6 has at times caused me to strive for an unrealistic perfection to keep people from seeing my 6. All the while, my relief came in embracing my 6 and not running from it. It is a part of me, and each time you encounter me, you encounter my 6.

But I have also realized that more than my 6 when you meet me, you experience what has truly helped me overcome. Some others in this world scored a 6 on that survey, and they became what the statistics said they would. Even though I didn't, I am no better than them. I could have gone the way of my 6 as well. There but for the grace of God go I. You see, I have overcome not by my strength but by the strength of the one who is the definition of the overcomer.

When my 6 tries to interfere with the plans and purposes God has for my life, when it tries to interrupt the straightway that the Lord has made for me, I don't have to engage in a façade of strength that ultimately wants to paralyze me. I just listen for the voice of the Lord to say, "My grace is sufficient for you, for My strength is made perfect in weakness".

Reverend Angela M. Tate currently serves as Associate Pastor of Westside Missionary Baptist Church. She received her Bachelor of Arts degree in Psychology from Maryville University and her Master of Education in Counseling from the University of Missouri-St Louis.

Angela is a licensed professional counselor (LPC) and has over 20 years of experience in non-profit leadership. She owns a counseling practice and serves as an adjunct faculty member of Harris Stowe State University.

Angela is a sought-after conference speaker and workshop facilitator. She often speaks about self-care, leadership, suicide prevention and mental health, and the Church. Angela's passion is seeing people healed through the power of faith in Jesus Christ and understands He uses counselors and therapists as instruments of His healing. She believes that sometimes the answer to our prayers is an excellent therapist.

She and her husband, Steve, have two young adult daughters and one granddaughter.

www.facebook.com/angela.montgomerytate
www.linkedin.com/in/amtateLPC
www.instagram.com/angela_m_tate

Devon Moody-Graham

Overcoming Yourself: Redefining You

Even before you were conceived, you were defined by the thoughts of your parents, their parents, friends, neighbors, and people you may never meet. These definitions and expectations can have more of an impact on your life than you realize. Usually, it isn't until we are approaching young adulthood that we realize that many of the choices we have made were based on what we assumed people wanted or expected of us. However, at some point, we have to define ourselves by ourselves, taking every other opinion with a grain of salt.

I have spent the last 18 years redefining who I was, based on a path that I would never have planned for myself so early in life, motherhood. However, I am a blessed and proud mother who has raised six and given birth to 4 amazing children. I never thought that I would have such a large family, and I never thought that a wife and mother of so many children could accomplish so much in life in such a short time.

Let's start with my Plan A. As a junior in college, majoring in Consumer and Textile Marketing, I had mapped out my post-undergraduate position as a Management and Merchandising Trainee for The May Company. I had worked at Famous Barr since I was 16 until my college years. I dreamt of moving to New York to take the fashion world by storm.

I had planned to study abroad before I completed my degree, and I was definitely NOT thinking about being a mother, a wife, or anything else that might keep me from reaching my goals.

It was May 2004, I was taking summer classes, working, and my then-boyfriend was visiting me in school. It was late evening, as we turned into Applebee's parking lot to get something to eat, I got a call that would forever change my life. My niece, aka my little sister, had been in a serious car accident, was unconscious, and in a coma. My sister made me promise not to drive home that night to avoid another possible accident and I waited until daybreak to get on the road for the longest ride home to be with my family.

When I got home, I knew that I couldn't go back to school because I wouldn't be able to concentrate, so I dropped my summer classes. Most of this is a blur now because I later learned that my brain erased many of my traumatic memories, bit by bit, so that I would be able to function better. It's neither a good nor bad thing, but the truth.

Of course, the more emotional I was, the more time I spent with my then-boyfriend, who was about to leave for New York to pursue his music career. I was furious, but I tried to be supportive until I wasn't. His departure was met with hurt, loneliness, and constant arguing until enough was enough. We broke up over the phone. I felt free. Shortly after, I visited my cousin in Chicago. One evening, we got dressed up and headed to a nightclub. I danced like it was my last night to dance, I had a blast! I started to overheat, felt sick to my stomach, and started to sweat more than normal as my stomach tightened. I was convinced it was something that I had eaten earlier and ran to the restroom. My cousin followed me, and as

I wiped water over my face, she said, "You're pregnant." I looked puzzled and laughed. She was already the mother of a beautiful little girl, so she knew what she was talking about, but I didn't listen.

I drank some water and went back out to the dance floor, but I didn't feel well for the rest of the night. I tried to enjoy myself, but all I could think about was the fact that I had been on birth control even before having sex because my mother didn't want me to be a teen mother. I also knew I had missed a couple pills. My nerves got the best of me by the time I made it back home. I took the "test" and it was positive. I was devastated but not defeated. After telling my parents, I promised myself and the baby growing inside me that I would do all I could to reach my goals.

This is my story of REDEFINED. Plan B.

A major part of redefining my story is identifying the false narrative that pregnancy destroys your plan and that mothers should no longer work toward their goals and dreams, but move toward a practical life that can support their child(ren). That could not be more WRONG. We have to replace false narratives with our OWN truth.

I am so blessed to have a supportive family that helped me successfully complete my first degree with my two-month-old son in the crowd. I welcomed my first child, Gregory, into the world, then I graduated from one of the top Universities in the country two months later. I enrolled in graduate school and completed my MBA as the mother of a toddler. After gaining great experience in marketing, and working long, inflexible hours, I decided to open my first consulting business — it was the best way to be available for my son. The journey of entrepreneurship was and still is a crazy roller-coaster ride, but I wouldn't trade the experience for anything.

I didn't know that part of my life's ministry would be to mothers, their hearts, unnecessary guilt, and hidden dreams. Each time I gave birth to a child, an amazing opportunity appeared, and I was forced to lose more and more of society's creation, "Mom Guilt." It is through my experiences that I have been able to help other mothers identify their feelings early. Your experiences matter, your WHY matters, your dreams matter, and your impact matters.

As a parent, I believe that my duty is to help my children think, dream, and do the impossible. I have never turned down an opportunity that God called me to, and he has never stopped calling me. I now remember my purpose-filled accomplishments in terms of how many children I had during the time. It's my testimony and blessing bookkeeping method, as a testament to what God can do no matter what even when your life takes a turn towards Plan B.

With One Child

- Graduated with my Bachelor of Science in Consumer and Textile Marketing
- Graduated with my MBA in less than two years
- Worked for the first black-owned beer company partnered with Anheuser Busch
- Started my first company

With 2 Children - 4 Children (Blended Family)

- Worked on my first commercial development grocery store

- Started first Independent Youth Golf Program at a black-owned golf course
- Selected as a speaker for Illinois Career Pathways Advocates
- Community representative to advocate for new area hospital while seven months pregnant

With 3 Children - 5 Children (Blended Family)

- Invited to the White House during President Barack Obama's Administration for my work in tech and entrepreneurship for Black youth
- Honored by the State of Illinois Comptroller for Black History Month
- Nationally honored for creating CEOMom to support mothers in life, business and career development
- With 4 Children- 6 Children (Blended Family)
- Spoke at the first women college in the United States, Mount Holyoke
- Planned first International Conference in Paris, France
- Assisted with Black Paris Community honoring Josephine Baker in Paris, France
- Featured in over 25 publications and a dozen podcasts, including 3 International
- Expanded Women's Experiences and College Student Immersion Program in Paris
- Planned Black Designer Focused Fashion Show in Paris, France
- Launched TV Show "Empire Talks" celebrating Legacy Building

Making it normal and necessary to celebrate wins no matter how big or small is a big part of my redefinition. Oftentimes, we downplay the magnitude or impact of our accomplishments when we should reflect on these moments when things are challenging.

After almost 17 years as a mother, God has continued to blow my mind by blessing me with opportunity after opportunity to give him the glory when God-sized dreams are answered amid life's challenges. So, if you are still wondering if you can still pursue your God-sized dreams, the answer is YES.

Even if you do not define yourself as a mother or a woman, this is still for you. If you have ever gotten out of bed when you didn't feel like it, you have overcome. If you have ever completed a task that you once thought was impossible, you have overcome. If you have ever defeated the odds that others stacked against you, you have overcome.

The Self-Definition journey is ongoing, and I am enjoying learning more about myself, my purpose, and the impact that I am supposed to leave along the way. I AM a woman, mother, wife, woman of God, daughter, community leader, author, serial entrepreneur, and international business strategist working to help others dust off the light that they have been dimming. Come on, we need your light to shine bright.

Keep overcoming!

Devon Moody-Graham is an international business strategist, impact speaker, and serial entrepreneur.

Devon is the Chief Solutions Officer of CEOMom Empire, which focuses on new market expansion for corporations and organizations and women's business development. She hosts business conferences globally to provide women with the tools to sustain and grow their businesses internationally.

With a heart for mothers, Devon's journey offers insight into overcoming the challenges of balancing your business while raising children. Her passion for the future took her to the White House in 2015 on the My Brother's Keeper STEM+ Roundtable with other game changers in entrepreneurship and technology. Devon's commitment to her client's success has helped them gross over $4 million+ in revenue and funding.

www.instagram.com/devonmoodygraham
www.linkedin.com/in/devonmoodygraham/
www.twitter.com/devonmoodygrahm
www.devonmoodygraham.com

Leslie Doyle

Never Defeated

*"You may encounter many defeats,
but you must not be defeated…"*

–Maya Angelou

My beloved grandmother, Claudean Daniel, taught many lessons, but I believe overcoming defeat was a lesson she exemplified best. After she passed in March 2019, I reflected on her life and the lessons she taught as I prepared to give her eulogy. She was an overcomer. Claudean Daniel's life mirrored the above quote by Maya Angelou. Although she faced many challenges, she was never defeated. My grandmother came from a long line of overcomers, and some may say, overachievers. Politician, teacher, CFO, and public servant are just a few of the titles people in my family possess because of a commitment to excellence.

Despite my grandmother's many challenges, she insisted that excellence be associated with her and everyone in her charge, especially our family. As the young people say, we understood the assignment because she drilled it into us. Grandma encouraged and reinforced striving to do our best. She was the family and the underdog's greatest cheerleader. Grandma traveled across the segregated South by station wagon to support her children in any competition and even abroad to other countries to cheer on her dear friends in the WNBA. She loved to see people win. Sometimes that success wasn't without conquering some serious obstacles.

While many in the family are trailblazers, achieving incredible highs, they also overcame unimaginable lows. As I reflected on my grandmother's life, I recalled not only the highs but the lows. She experienced a challenging childhood. She was raised by a relative who was not nurturing, and a mother living with her own grief and trauma. Grandma survived an abusive marriage and worked three jobs as a single mother of five children. Yes, she knew trials.

Circumstances, racism, and sexism threatened her potential many times. However, defeat did not define her. She never allowed herself to wallow in self-pity or anyone else. Famous for her football analogies (I mentioned her love of competition), she would often say: "You just gotta back up and punt!" For her, that meant reevaluating the angle and trajectory and trying again.

As I reflect on my life, I recall her sage advice whenever I face an obstacle. Wallowing in the shoulda-coulda-woulda halts forward movement. I have faced many forks in the road and decisions that altered my life's path from school and work to my personal life. I have always lived with faith that my steps are ordered and part of a larger plan. Indeed, life deals us defeat, but we must fight on. Some people have only heard the first part of the quote. The part that often is left off says, "In fact, it may be necessary to experience defeats, so you can know who you are, what you can rise from, how you can still come out of it."

The necessity of defeat is a part of the quote we sometimes forget. Nobody is excited about loss, but it is inevitable. Some of the greatest champions speak of defeat. Michael Jordan, the GOAT of basketball, talks about failure and how he used it to fuel his dreams. In a now famous commercial, he testifies about his losses, crediting them for his success. We must know defeat to understand overcoming. It may be hard to enumerate how many times we fail as Jordan does. Hopefully, it isn't as difficult to reflect on the lessons learned from defeat. The lessons of defeat are an essential element of success. It is not the number of shots missed (more than 9,000) or games lost (approximately 300) like Jordan, but the adjustments we make based on failure that leads to success.

As an educator, I've coached students through setbacks knowing that it was a part of their journey. Watching a student struggle is one of the hardest things to do, knowing you must allow them to figure it out for themselves. I have witnessed countless professional trajectory changes when they can't manage to pass an exam or a test. What I know is through those situations, they discover their true path.

Stacy Abrams' story typifies a person that learned from rejection. Her gubernatorial race seemingly ended with a stunning loss, or did it? Perhaps, her failure led to victory. Maybe she didn't have the personal outcome she desired yet, but she took those lessons and changed the course of the 2020 election. One magazine referred to her as "the most influential unelected politician." Fighting voter suppression in Georgia helped President Biden win the election and is heralded as a victory for Stacy, Georgia, and the Democratic Party. Stacy took the lessons of vanquishment and flipped them to understand she could rise and not be defined by her experience.

There are many lessons in defeat. Knowing who and whose you are in the midst of defeat is grounding. The oral tradition of storytelling is strong in our family. Those stories remind us who we are, where we come from, and what we are capable of accomplishing. They, too, remind us of the hopes and dreams of our ancestors, detailing how far we've come and all that is possible. I revel in hearing the tales of my ancestors that survived slavery, Jim Crow, and legal segregation. Harrowing stories of my five-time great grandmother having a finger cut off every time she was caught reading or how my great grandfather and his family had to flee the Tulsa Race Riots of 1921 cement the knowledge of who I am. We discuss our lineage frequently. The responsibility of being a descendent from a long line of overcomers is as grounding as my faith.

Faith has served as a cornerstone for my life and my family. Overcoming has biblical grounding as well. John 16:33 reads: "I have told you these things, so that in me you may have peace…In this world you will have trouble. …But take heart! I have overcome the world."

As children of the Most High, we can have confidence in knowing that we all must surrender eventually. The scripture calls us to take heart in knowing God is with us. Amid your trials, God calls us to a deeper relationship with Him by asking us to trust, lean, and depend on Him. We should exercise our faith in knowing that He plans to prosper us and not harm us. Ultimately, God is working for our good because He is our Father, and as such, there is no need to be afraid.

That faith and heritage, as God's people, has carried us for centuries. The story of Blacks is often told, with the beginning starting at slavery. Our story began before slavery. Africans were not just enslaved, people.

Often the story we hear starts with slavery, but the whole civilization existed for centuries before slavery. Africa produced brilliant minds and rich cultures.

From the enslavement of Africans and the subsequent subjugation through the official end of slavery through Jim Crow to the modern-day lynching at the hands of police and the prison-industrial complex, we have firmly cemented our place as overcomers and survivors. Blacks in America have survived time and time again from all of the systems and structures that work to perpetuate a caste system that provides greater access and resources to some while systematically denying it to others. Yet, we overcome every day. And, boy, do we do so with style and grace. The election of Former President Barack Obama to the highest office in the landmarked a pivotal moment in American history where a Black man triumphed over a system many deemed too far out of reach and a space many never thought they would see in their lifetimes. I wept watching him and First Lady Michelle Obama dance on inauguration night for all the things it symbolized.

In spite of the challenges I've had in my life, I've overcome them. Those challenges are an essential part of who I am. I was born to a teenage mom, molested, raised in the projects, a product of public schools, and surrounded by drugs and poverty. Kids living in my zip code were not expected to go to college, let alone earn four college degrees, speak on stages about the power of diversity or accompany thousands of young people on their journey to becoming. It has been important for me to shatter the existing ceilings and let down the ladder for those after me.

I am thankful for defeat. Without tests, there would be no testimony. Those things taught me who I was and that I could rise from any challenge. Indeed, I have experienced defeat, and I'll never be defeated. Thank you, Grandma, for the lessons learned and the life you led that reminds us to keep striving!

Leslie Doyle, Ed. D. is the Interim Director of the Office of Student Diversity & Social Justice (SDSJ) at Las Vegas University of Nevada.

She began her career at the University of Kansas (KU) in 1997 as a Hall Director and program coordinator, followed by joining Nebraska Wesleyan University in October 1999 as the Multicultural Student Coordinator. In 2005, she left this post to join Fontbonne University as the Director of Multicultural Affairs, later promoted to the Director of Service, Diversity, and Social Justice. Following the death of Mike Brown in St. Louis in 2014, Dr. Doyle began leading strategic diversity and inclusion efforts for Fontbonne University. In April 2019, Dr. Doyle became the inaugural Chief Inclusion Officer at Rockhurst University.

Doyle earned a Bachelor of Science at Northwest Missouri State University, a Master of Science in higher education at the University of Kansas, a Master of Management in business and leadership at Fontbonne University, and a Doctor of Education in higher education leadership at Maryville University.

Outside of higher education, she has served as a consultant and speaker to various organizations focusing on equity. Her work spans multiple industries, including healthcare, nonprofits, and religious institutions.

www.facebook.com/leslie.doyle.56

linkedin.com/in/dr-leslie-doyle-she-her-hers-a739bab7

Vanessa Cooksey

The Three Ds of My PPP

In 1997, my dad died from pancreatic cancer. I was 19 years old. He was my best friend, and I was devastated. I thought that was the worst thing that could ever happen to me. In 2008, I didn't get a promotion that I worked hard to earn, and I thought that was the worst thing that could ever happen to me. But, in 2020, my child spent the last two months of second grade learning at home. Let me tell you, that was the worst thing that ever happened to me!

The pandemic has had distressing impacts on all of us, from increased anxiety to job loss and even death. Like you, I spent a lot of time at home, and my day-to-day routines were disrupted entirely. The pandemic gave me a unique opportunity to rethink many things and establish and live in a new normal. Motivated by my friend, Lauren, and encouraged by my cousin, Demetria, to find hope and power in vulnerability, I took time in the early months of the pandemic to develop a Post-Pandemic Playbook (PPP). I even gave a speech about it during a virtual Women's Day event at my church and developed it into a webinar for the National Council of Negro Women. Like most people, I had hoped the pandemic would be over by the end of the year, and I wanted to be ready for how the world would change as a result of it. Now, two years later, as the pandemic has evolved, so has my perspective. My playbook is more of a permanent mindset, a Pandemic Preparedness Playbook that helps me navigate the never-ending volatility, uncertainty, complexity, and ambiguity that we live with every day. I hope after reading this, you are inspired to develop your own PPP.

I have three principles that serve as the foundation of my playbook. I fondly call them the three Ds. The first "D" in my playbook is a personal pledge to be **debt-free**. My commitment to good stewardship is directly related to my belief in self-determination. Achieving and maintaining financial stability is paramount to overcoming any crisis. Anyone who has ever borrowed money can relate to the scripture, "the borrower is slave to the lender."

> *Debt comes with its own hardship and tends to make crises more severe.*

While I am not debt-free yet, I work to limit unproductive and excessive debt. I love radio talk show host Joe Madison's quote, "the difference between a moment and a movement is sacrifice." Overcoming the bondage of debt requires me to be disciplined and sacrifice my desire for instant gratification in support of long-term investing and wealth building.

I started working my senior year in high school, and I didn't save any of that hard-earned money. I drove it, wore it, and ate it all up! When I went to college, I continued working and spending. My mom discouraged me from getting a credit card. My parents didn't talk to me directly about debt when I was a child, so her warning seemed a little out of left field, but I listened anyway. However, when I graduated from college, got my first "real job," and determined I was "grown," I signed up for every credit card I could get. It was then that I experienced the real burden of revolving consumer debt as I tried to make ends meet on a modest entry-level salary. In the early years of my career, I made job choices based on money versus purpose to keep up with my debt payments. Changing my relationship with money took a lot of time and study. Now, when I have the opportunity to connect with young adults, I share my annual Social Security earnings statement, and I encourage them to save and invest money while they're young. I caution them that saving and managing money gets more challenging and complex with age and more responsibility.

My playbook's second "D" is a personal pledge to be **disease-free**. Taking care of my health is as important as taking care of my wealth. I've witnessed six virus-related pandemics during my lifetime (HIV/AIDS, Ebola, SARS, etc.). I am also concerned with the chronic disease epidemic in our country. According to the United States Centers for Disease Control and Prevention (CDC), 6 out of 10 Americans have a chronic disease such as heart disease, cancer, and diabetes. These are the leading causes of death and disability in the United States.

I have struggled with weight for most of my adult life. It got more challenging in my thirties and worse after I married and my child was born. In February of 2019, as I approached my 42nd birthday, I was sick and tired of being sick and tired. I also had to admit that by medical definition, I was in the obese category, and I was desperate for a transformative lifestyle change. I started nutrition coaching, and I purchased my first Tower Garden. I began growing herbs, fruits, and vegetables at home indoors and outdoors year-round. When the pandemic started just over a year later and shut down restaurants and limited access to grocery stores, I remember sitting in my kitchen, looking at my Tower Garden, and thanking God that I could feed my family healthy food despite any disruption to the food supply chain.

Investing in nutrition coaching was critical to my health transformation. Like the executive coaches that I've partnered with to support my professional growth and development, one-on-one wellness coaching provided the accountability that I needed to help me change my perspective on how I was caring for my mind, body, and spirit. Much of what I learned about nutrition over the years was inaccurate or irrelevant. My coach challenged me to learn how to eat to live versus live to eat. The one thing I treasure most from working with a coach is that he helped me develop a personal health affirmation. It keeps me motivated to stay the course despite any setbacks that I experience. Even though I have it memorized, I still read it every morning, 'I commit to being fully present today, and I nourish my body for maximum wellness.' I founded Vested Urban Farms because I am passionate about health and wellness. Vested Urban Farms is a tech-assisted farming company that grows fresh, nutrient-rich fruits, vegetables, and herbs in urban communities. Our tower gardens, tower farms, and community engagement programs connect like-minded people with plant-powered personal nutrition and entrepreneurship opportunities.

The third "D" in my playbook is a personal pledge to be **drama-free**. One of my favorite pastimes is looking through photo albums. I love taking pictures. I've captured thousands of unforgettable moments with my friends, family, and coworkers. I also spend time reading my old journals. The time I spend with my journals and photo albums shows me how I've grown and matured over the years. I admit most of the drama I've experienced has been caused by self-imposed nonsense. The unrealistic expectations I have of myself and others, coupled with my desire to be recognized as a generous, hard-working, and likable person (also known as the "good girl" syndrome), often resulted in my being disappointed, stressed, and overwhelmed. I can't count the number of times I said YES to something or someone when I really should have said NO. Sometimes we experience more drama in our lives when a crisis hits because we don't have any extra bandwidth or capacity to slow down, think and respond, so we just react.

Today, I control the drama in my life by making choices aligned with my core values: creativity and well-being. Once I affirmed my life's purpose, I set realistic emotional boundaries and committed to a daily spiritual practice. The drama I experienced internally and externally lessened each day and was replaced by an inexplicable sense of peace.

I accept with gratitude that where I am right now is where I am supposed to be. Everything I've had to overcome prepared me for greater relationships, rewards, and responsibility. There are two key benefits of developing a personal pandemic preparedness playbook. The first benefit is that preparedness limits suffering. Because I am upright and breathing, I know that challenges are inevitable. At any given moment, I try to be aware of my proximity to a "life storm": (1) going into a storm, (2) being in the storm, or (3) coming out of a storm. Having a plan and principles that guide the things that I can control and navigate the things I cannot control makes going through a crisis of any kind (big or small) more bearable.

The most important benefit of having a playbook is that my playbook positions me to win. Winning sports teams have great playbooks to help them win championships. A playbook can do the same for you.

Being debt-free, disease-free, and drama-free can help us win the game of life. We CAN win. We can win with ourselves, our families, our careers, and our communities!

And Lord knows we deserve to win.

As Founder & CEO of Vested Urban Farms, Vanessa Cooksey is committed to helping people live their best lives through plant-powered nutrition and healthy lifestyles. Deeply impacted by her father's death from pancreatic cancer, she aligned her efforts with the Juice Plus (JP) Company in 2019 and quickly grew in the organization by building a national team of residential Tower Garden partners and customers. In 2020, she received the JP Team Builder award. She is currently leading the Regional Arts Commission of St. Louis.

Vanessa has more than 25 years of business and civic leadership experience, including Mary Kay Cosmetics, The City of Atlanta Mayor's Office, Cartoon Network, Anheuser Busch, and Wells Fargo. She has served on several local and national nonprofit boards, including the SIFMA Foundation for Investor Education, Harris-Stowe State University, Vote Run Lead, and Mercy Health. She is also a proud member of Delta Sigma Theta Sorority, Inc. Vanessa has received over 60 awards for her industry and community impact, including the 2016 Eisenhower Fellowship and the 2018 St. Louis American Corporate Executive of the Year Award.

Vanessa earned her bachelor's degree in Radio-Television-Film from the University of Texas at Austin, a master's degree in Business Administration from Webster University. Vanessa enjoys cycling, cooking, and spending quality time with her friends and family.

www.vestedurbanfarms.com
www.linkedin.com/in/vlafc

Kynisha Ducre

Life in a Magical Box

In 2022, women's roles have shifted considerably from 40 and 60 years ago. African American and African women are some of THE most educated demographics in the United States. (*Yes, you can give some pride-filled finger snaps to that*). Our determination and well-surviving instincts are stellar. Yet, some of us are often ill-advised to stay in one lane, like there isn't an entire four-lane highway we can carefully navigate to get to our destination. Many factors can cause us to shift lanes like intentional selection, speed desired, or response to unexpected construction and lane closures (*Read that again, figuratively*)! Just buckle up, keep your hands on the wheel, and enjoy the ride.

Growing up in New Orleans with 16 maternal aunts and uncles, I have seen life played out in a myriad of ways. With over 50 cousins, there was always someone comparing us as kids. Though I was sometimes placed on a pedestal due to age, my mom's matriarch role, and determination, I felt odd in my own big family.

I loved a good story, liked animal shows, international culture, geography, and the history of the Bible. So, stories like Joseph and his coat of many colors, being sold by his brothers because of jealousy, then welcoming his family in spite of and reuniting with his dad moved me. Or, like David, who lived simply as a young man, yet was rewarded for his dedication in the small things, having to hide, becoming king, etc., were all fascinating.

Fast forward to humbly realizing talents I seem to have. I genuinely felt magical as a kid and a teen. Somewhere between my early teenage years and young adult life, I was told to focus on one thing to excel in. I was confused by that because there were singers who also acted, ballplayers who had franchises, and hairdressers that operated boutiques. Something finally clicked that some people could only see what was in front of them and not beyond. So, with a spiritual gift of ignoring, I continued to explore interest with curiosity to flip through the encyclopedia to find out more. (*Encyclopedias were like a mini Google within alphabetized books, FYI*).

I vividly remember a time when a family member was dismissive about a major high school accomplishment of mine. Being accepted into a performing arts school was no easy feat in the '80s. What stung most was she had no idea how much I had prepared, prayed, practiced, and overcame my insecurities to be selected. Like, why wasn't celebrating the first thing out of her mouth? (*Sometimes your own family is the worst, right?*) I ignored it, for the most part, clipped the picture and article out of the local newspaper, and push-pinned it to my wall. From that point on, I listened more than I spoke and dimmed my glow for others' comfort.

At that moment, I learned how to manipulate bad energy into good and be guided by my parents, supportive neighbors, friends, teachers, and church family. (*#blessed*) As naïve and magical as I was, I often quoted Mary Poppins, "Everything is possible." My favorite Bible verse is Galatians 6:4-5 (MSG) "*Make a careful exploration of who you are and the work you have been given and then sink yourself into that. Don't be impressed* with yourself. Don't compare yourself with others. Each of you must take responsibility for doing the creative best you can with your own life." Bible verses truly humble me.

From that dancing achievement, I went on to cheer and dance in high school, college, and even the NFL for the New Orleans Saints. (*Who Dat Baaabey!*) The moral of that story is don't let a person without vision dictate your next move, and don't be that person to blur someone else's path. Just like an eyeglass prescription is based on your specific measurements of clarity, God has crafted custom lenses (and dreams) just for you. Many have experienced 20/20 clarity and insight in the stillness of His grace. My vision and focus have been to inspire people, especially kids, to see themselves as God does.

I graduated with a Bachelor's of Science Degree in Psychology/Chemistry from a New Orleans HBCU and an Associates of Arts in Interior Design. After receiving the interior design degree, I worked at a fabric store, high-end furniture gallery, architectural firm, commercial furniture dealer. I then landed the interior design role at my first alma mater, Xavier University of Louisiana. There, I worked on classroom design, the university center, ecclesiastical spaces, dormitories, science/pharmaceutical laboratories, and the 'mighty Greek yard', which was indeed amazing!

Now, I create magical spaces as a licensed Interior Design manager with a crew of 100-plus for one of the 'Best Places to Work' in Silicon Valley. And this client is well known for creative spaces and a rainbow culture of excellence spanning more than 200 buildings in the Bay Area alone. *(#proud)*

Let's break down the ladder climb to my professional career and the faith to trust! I honestly never dreamed about being a "boss," but I did want to inspire and lead others well. Even in writing this chapter, I reflect that being teachable, asking for input, and humility are indeed a winning trifecta. Sprinkles of joy, a portion of confident boundaries, and a side of integrity will also allow you to thrive.

There will always be disrespect attempted, microaggressions to overcome (*with the time needed to give for that day*), racism to intellectually uncover, unfulfilled promises, bogus HR write-ups, insecure moments, knowledge to gain in your free time, and strength to adjust your crown!

What did I miss? Oh, tears to cry, health, financial, and love loss too. Continue reading chapters of *this book* or be open to therapy for true overcoming.

We all have had and will continue to have failures, but stop seeing them as the end of the road and more as a detour to your destiny. How will we learn besides understanding what didn't work, asking better questions, or analyzing and strategizing differently? Random thought: Have you ever watched Shark Tank and studied the product setup, story delivery, financial statistics, and number crunching anticipated when it was time to consider a partnership? It took research, commitment to learning/knowing your market, and infrastructure to capture said data. Or, if speaking is your #goal, watch Ted Talks, get your formatting ready, and start memorizing a little per day. You have magic, too!

Many of us have heard the saying, "A jack of all trades is a master of none, but often better than a master of one." When you have an entrepreneurial spirit, find yourself wanting to change careers, or make extra money, you have to pull from all your gifts, educate yourself and do it. You have to start somewhere and be consistent. Solicit accomplished goal-getters who can help you assess your strengths, then invest in a coach, conference or attend YouTube University to soar confidently. We all have learned to juggle things without even realizing it and have a plethora of undiscovered skill sets. Remain prayerful, teachable, and elevate over your doubt. When you can, watch the movies *Hidden Figures* or *The Greatest Showman* to see examples of people taking a leap to expand creatively.

Though my interior design career pays the bills, my true passion lies in being a professionally trained, yet naturally silly clown. Yes, you read that right (*glitter nose, balloon twisting, and fly clown shoes too*)! As Daisy the Clown™, I'm humbled to entertain kids and adults across the globe. While this literal juggling takes lots of concentration, our lives and goals do too. There was no relatable book to catapult my "Clownin' Around," but I chartered my own course and taught myself who and how I wanted to be. This smile has traveled to 6 continents and 33 countries, and graced magazines. Yet, spreading joy is serious business for this clown. For years, I served in children's church doing gospel clowning, which prepared me to publish a Biblical Guide with balloon twisting fun, entitled, "Create in Me!"

The pandemic has significantly delayed Daisy's book tour, but I won't complain about the additional planning for the extra coordination needed. And making better use of my time to focus/learn from others' success helped my positive mindset. I can't wait to offer my first balloon twisting class and book signing soon! (**Daisy The Clown has free Affirmation**

Alphabets, clown shows with balloon twisting, magical moments, now on YouTube.)

My flower-child mindset has carried me for decades, with God leading my steps. You cannot always contain a glow, nor should you want to. Be honest with yourself, seek improvement, and realize your organization, schedule, time wasters, research, and pray with expectancy. Faith of a mustard seed, 'me-time' and a sound mind are musts! (*And we are not giving up ok.*)

I have questioned and now concluded that there IS NOT a customizable box we fit in. Goods and services can indeed be placed in a nicely branded box, but WE, my friends, are just too magical!

As a true, southern charm and well-traveled collective of experiences, Kynisha Ducre is living an amazing adventure!

Being goal-driven as a child, excelling personally and professionally throughout the decades has been fulfilling. The constant juggling, jumping through hoops of fire, balancing acts while being the ringmaster to keep everyone engaged, smiling, and excited has been quite the circus! Though Kynisha is an internationally award-winning clown known as DaisyTheClown™, maintaining balance has been a skill needing the most preparation.

Kynisha holds degrees in psychology and interior design. She leads interior design and space management vendors for one of the largest tech companies in the Bay Area. And though that corporate climb has seemed like walking a tightrope at times, mental toughness is the biggest overcomer coupled with prayer and coaching/therapy!

No matter the circus you currently find yourself in, let's get through this together.

www.youtube.com/user/daisy75070

www.instagram.com/daisytheclown/

Ronke Faleti

Future Pride: The Courage to Overcome

"I have four kids."

This is a statement of fact that I frequently utter — at times with pride — and at other times with trepidation of judgment. I never expected these four words to be a plea for surviving. With both of my hands up in the position of surrender, I said in a quaking and calm voice, "I have four kids."

The recipient of my words was one of two armed robbers at the cell phone store I walked into shortly after 7 p.m. on Saturday, September 4, the day humanity paused to celebrate Beyoncé turning 40.

The gunman's unmasked accomplice personified fear parading back and forth in the open saying "Don't do anything stupid." With a light tap to my shoulder, he pronounced in a firm, yet sincere tone: "Don't do anything stupid, you gon' be alright!" It was then that I looked him in the face and said, "I have four kids."

Flight. Fight. Freeze.

My life did not flash before my eyes. The faces of my four children did not appear in my mind. Getting home to continue to mother the four was my sole prayer point even without an explicit ask. I wondered if this was the moment to slyly reach for my phone and press record. I decided against moving my hands, as this could be the 'something stupid' and kept them visibly up. I did not scream. I did not cry. I did not move. I did not even feel the weakness I normally feel in my knees when I experience sudden fear. I was frozen in time with clarity of purpose: **get home**.

Danger dissipated after the two thieves of funds and freedom walked out through the same doors that chimed in announcement of their arrival just minutes before. I wept breathlessly. The young associate who was previously lying facing down, came toward me — looked into my eyes; read my soul and began to coach me on breathing exercises. I locked my eyes on him and shook in fear. He said, "Breathe with me; breathe with me and thank God we're here." That minute we took breathing together felt like I experienced saving grace. It felt like an angel reached into the fragility of my soul and whispered to me, "You're safe: I've got you. It's gonna be okay."

I drove home.

I prostrated myself in praise and worship of the Almighty One who saw fit that I should witness danger and not be damaged. As promised and recorded in the songs of David, "He lifted me up on eagle's wings, lest I dash my foot against a stone."

I was overcoming.

This experience led me to ask myself, **"When will I do His will?"**

The nagging and nascent "YES, God" that lay in dormancy awakened. Will I be buried with His treasure because I lack sufficient courage to act? I asked myself, "Why am I languishing?" Having avoided an untimely and permanent gravesite address where "never birthed" treasures lay, I faced up to the truth — I am not courageous enough to live in discomfort. *I play small for fear of community rejection*.

The past is prologue.

Cliques of community scare me.

It wasn't until I sat down across from a friend who does therapy for entrepreneurs that I began to see the chains from my past — the ones I log around as anchors holding me back from my future. "What would the Africans say? What would they say!?" are the words I kept repeating defiantly in defense of my fear to put myself 'out there.' My friend, Jewish and not African, pressed on and asked, "Are Africans not entrepreneurial?" Au contraire, mon ami. We are the hustle masters! Her words after hearing my story were "Oooh, I get it: you felt ostracized by your community." For the first time in more than 20 years, hearing those strings of words opened my eyes to see the shackles I'd placed on myself and helped me to unlock a cheat code to my freedom.

After arriving at a new high school my sophomore year, the legend of "the other African girl you should meet" emerged, and it became my mission to meet and befriend her. By the second semester, we were BFFs! She, 15 and me, 364 days younger. We did what most teenage girls do — talk on the phone a lot with boys as our favorite and most studious subject. In the season of our best-friends forever status, her grades and teenage antics began to dip below the acceptable immigrant standard of excellence. The African instinct of her parents to clamp down went into full force and my "bad company" was their logical explanation.

Like wildfire, word began to spread in the community. The African elders came to brand me as a cautionary warning to their children:

my contemporaries. I learned, from a friend on a visit to an African parents' home, that the customary "good-girl praises" I'd come to enjoy were replaced with "do not associate yourself with that girl." In another instance, my mother was at a wedding when other unfamiliar mothers at the table began to whisper, "Which one of them is that Ronke girl?" These words landed on my mother's ears and turned into tears falling from her eyes. "You are a mamiwata" translated to "you are bewitched — an evil beauty" are words I heard firsthand from the family that branded me as such. Those words, and many others like them, mildly itch today, but 22 years ago, they were grenades that shattered my very being.

Withdrawing from community was my soul's solace.

Tight-knit communities started to feel dangerous. I began to cultivate the habit of playing small to not offend. I furthered my own ostracization even when I genuinely sought to be part of the crew. I latched on, with expectancy, to the pain of rejection. I limited my entrepreneurial growth and became flighty in personal relationships. Hearing "you felt ostracized by *your* community" unlocked years of programming that was doing me a disservice. I realized that I **get** to choose triumph or fear. "What would people say?" was replaced with, "Will I unabashedly pursue His will?"

I am overcoming.

His Will for Me: Build Community

On December 20, 2020, the last Sunday of Advent, I attended church for the first time since the beginning of the pandemic. The sermon was about Mary's *yes* being the beginning of my Christian faith. The priest explained that saying yes to one's **great calling** is the beginning of happiness. I wrote myself in a notebook I carried with me, "What am I not saying yes to?" Immediately, the word "mother" flew into my head and heart with a knowing sense. "For more women to choose motherhood???" are the words I wrote down. It's the calling I've run from since I launched korédé, a line of leather bags for women, three years prior. I whispered in my soul "*yes…ish.*"

Things Fall Apart. Now What?

I asked my 83-year-old father to share with me a story of his "overcoming." He told me of his determination to come to America and highlighted the ingredients to overcome anything:

You must have a goal

You must have iforiti. *Iforiti*: courageous perseverance in pursuit of one's goal

You must believe in yourself.

I assessed why months had turned into a year and yet, the whispered yes to the call from God remained yes..*ish*.

What is the goal?

A space where community happens, a better place to hide, a gathering space for mothers. A place for commerce, capital, crisis abatement, community gathering, rest, restorative care, and hope.

Better outcomes for families, less trauma in the world, mothers thriving, in community and not competition!? Whoa! Is this God's restorative justice? Me, a runner from community to help establish community? Wow!

Iforiti

The courage it takes to start, share, promote, partner, employ remains tiring and at times insurmountable. I busied myself in decks and spreadsheets to show activity but achieved no real progress and faced minimal discomfort. "Iforiti" demands discomfort of putting yourself out there.

On the morning of November 12, 2021 — this happened… I can't make this up. I woke up, used the restroom; walking back to my bed, a book fell of the bookshelf. I stepped back to look at the Bible and it had opened to Joshua.

> *"Have I not commanded you? Be strong and of good courage; do not be afraid, nor be dismayed, for the Lord your God is with you wherever you go."*
>
> *– Joshua 1:9*

Be strong and Courageous!

Believing in myself — my biggest challenge yet.

I don't have *that* kind of money. I am the income earner in our current sandwiched family of our nuclear six and my elderly parents. And, what would people say!? Here she goes again with another "idea."

Then there's the guilt I associate with bigging myself up when it comes to 'believing in myself". How do I overcome this guilt and know that I am #amazing? Where do I top off courage? Is there a number to call?

The gaze of admiration, vindication, even envy from those who branded me bad, no longer worked as a motivator. I question if I have what it takes to go out there and will into existence a wellness space for mothers and better outcomes for our society. The self-talk of "Who am I to do this?" did not have the confident response of "the child of the Almighty and heir to the throne." It was more along the lines of, "Who do you think you are?"

I needed a script: I landed on **Future Pride** as the prescription. This, as told to me by my father, is how you borrow belief. Future Pride held by me and others in this generation and the ones to come is the system of belief I choose over fear of rejection.

To overcome, ask yourself what discomforts
you lack the courage to experience?

I know that following a vision that was provided to just me will appear distorted to others. On my way, I will be met with tremendous discomfort and resistance that will surely demand activation of divine "iforiti." Overcoming implies a known hardship. Hiding and withdrawing were tools for a 15-year-old girl, courage is a choice for this 38-year-old woman determined to shake the world into creating better outcomes for our first teachers and shapers of society: our mothers.

Overcomers belong to the community of dream-birthers that change all of our tomorrows. On Beyonce's 40th birthday, I was reminded of my pending initiation into that community. In writing and publishing this piece, I humbly submit my application.

Ronke Faleti is a storyteller.

She launched korédé, inc. in 2018, as a leather handbag line that merged beauty with function. In 2022, she launched the I A.M. Summit by korédé as a gathering oasis delivering restorative care and wisdom through storytelling for ambitious and courageous mothers.

Ronke has been married to Yinka Faleti for almost 12 years, and together, they shepherd the lives of Fisayo, Tiwa, Sade, and Motunrayo. "Mother" is the most consequential and fragile title she holds, the one that humbles her and the one that makes her proudest.

Ronke was born and raised in Nigeria and at age eleven, emigrated with her family to Texas. She spent her secondary and college education years in Arlington, Texas and matriculated from University of Texas in Arlington. She has been a financial professional for 14 years with a major national brokerage Firm.

In her spare time, she enjoys doing life with her family, listening to audiobooks, writing, and hosting gatherings.

www.twitter.com/ronke_faleti
www.linkedin.com/in/ronkefaleti/
www.futurepridejournal.com
iamsummit.org
ronke@korede.co

Sherry Sissac

Overcoming the Yes Syndrome

It was 2015, the year I picked up Shonda Rhimes' *New York Times* Best Seller book, *The Year of Yes*. I'd always been a huge fan of Shonda, this incredibly talented producer, writer, a creator who has shaken up network television — a consummate storyteller, although some of the storylines were a bit fantastic. She's fierce, innovative, and a card-carrying member of badassery. A real game-changer who's still calling the shots, she's known for being intentional about casting women, people of color, and people of the LGBTQ community in roles that reflect the world as it is.

A fan of Shonda's works, *Grey's Anatomy*, *Scandal*, and *Private Practice*, I didn't hesitate to buy her book. It was a quick read, insightful, funny, and relatable. As a black working mom who grew up with similar sensibilities as Shonda's, I couldn't wait to read her perspective on life and career. While my years in television dwarf Shonda's successes, we both were single working moms, juggling the demands of career and home.

As a working mom, life issues were non-stop. The only thing I knew to do was keep all the balls up in the air. There was never an option to let any ball hit the ground. Band practice. Check! (Jazz, Marching, and Orchestra!) Parent-teacher conferences. Check! Doctors' appointments. Check! Field trips. Check! Science projects. Check! Homework reviews. Check! Grocery shopping. Check! Prepare breakfast. Lunch. Dinner.

Check! Check! Check! Church on Sunday. Check! Community service. Check!

And then there was my job. When I started my career at a large Chicago ad agency, I was one of only a few African American media/buyer planners and the only person of color assigned to one of their largest clients. I showed up ready to prove I was smart and could consistently perform at a high level. I said yes to every assignment and frequently volunteered to lead employee engagement activities. It was the beginning of my professional road of firsts and onlies — the *first* black woman to serve in this role or the *only* black woman to lead that project. I needed to prove to my colleagues that I was qualified, a team player, and good enough to be here. I was determined never to let them see me sweat.

Years later, when I joined a healthcare organization, I was thrilled to finally secure a well-deserved corner office, but I was careful about bringing any evidence of what might appear to be a hindrance or a distraction. There were no pictures of my kids or other personal effects in my office — how foolish it was not to bring my entire self to work. I was compensated for my hard work but never compensated for the sacrifices I made. I BLAMED MYSELF when I didn't receive a certain promotion or glowing performance review. I thought I didn't work hard enough, long enough, or tough enough. Never once considering the inequities, office politics, and flat-out racist behaviors I and others were experiencing. I believed myself to be exceptional, casting a naïve blind eye to what was going on.

Work became my priority. And for everything else outside of work, I was always too busy or never quite fully present. I was checking the boxes to get shit done, and like a bad habit, I moved into a position to do it all over again the next day. I was always off to the next thing while solving everybody's problems. I spent my entire career on the presupposition that to have anything worth something in life, the only answer was to say yes. Raise your hand. Be the first one in. Jump at the chance, as it might not ever come again. As a kid, my dad said, "There are two people in the world, leaders and followers. Be a leader." This conditioning was central to my professional life.

I was "that" woman. Divorced. Single. Mom of four. Problem solver. The always-there-for you-last-minute-bake-the-cookies-for-the-school-bake-sale-call-me-anytime-I-can-do-it-and-will-have-it-on-your-desk-in-the-morning wonder woman. I was exhausted!

This default practice of saying yes constantly was slowly suffocating me. I became resentful, anxious, and overly protective of my time to the point that I began refusing invitations from friends and family to have a moment to breathe. Early on, I didn't recognize how troubling this behavior was to my health and spirit. I thought this was expected of me as a working mom.

I was a caring, considerate, and empathetic person but never characterized as a people pleaser. I was a decisive, outcomes-based leader and a self-prescribed problem solver, with an innate belief that there's always a solution to almost any problem at home or work. And I was the person to fix it. How misguided. How delusional. In later years, I learned a sobering lesson — sometimes there are no solutions, and the best thing and the only thing we can do is to choose how we respond to circumstances that are out of our control.

Shonda's *Year of Yes* was all about having the courage to step outside her comfort zone and embrace being vulnerable to the world. Because of her courage to step into who she is, her life flourished. As I reflect on Shonda's book of YES, I discovered an even greater power. Rather than saying yes to things that appeared intriguing or daunting, I learned to believe in the power of no. Making this transition from yes to no has been a process.

A dear friend once said to me, "Saying no to one thing opens opportunities for other things that are needed now in your life, right now." It doesn't mean that I'm blindly saying no to everything that may or may not be an opportunity but saying "no" now helps me choose what is necessary and most beneficial for my family and me. Saying no has become my guiding principle. It has allowed me to be more discerning. To create boundaries and deepen my time with others. Saying no and leaning into it doesn't diminish the person I have become. Saying no allowed me to let others shine.

Saying no means doing less but amplifying my yes. It helps me declutter and get rid of all the busy stuff that doesn't please my soul or make my heart sing. It's about saying no to things that don't serve me and saying yes to things that do. Sometimes, we get to choose ourselves. That's not a bad thing. Saying no has made me stronger. Saying no has allowed me to strengthen my relationship with my friends and family. My most important job in the world is to be the best mom I can be. When I worked late nights and weekends, my mother would constantly remind me, "You are replaceable at work, but you are not replaceable at home." As leaders, we need to mirror what is important for our kids and our work community. We must lead by example.

For me, saying yes didn't hold the promise of success or fulfillment. Perhaps I was saying yes to too many of the wrong things. Maybe it was fear of losing control. As black women, we have been conditioned to make a way out of no way. It has been our badge of honor. We pride ourselves on being able to do it all, both at home and at the office. We believe our responsibility is to put others first with the promise that we'll get back to us later. But we never do. We believe we should fix everything. At home. At work. And then we become known as these superwomen who can do it all.

We set that expectation for others to witness as we struggle inside to figure out a way to sustain it. This is not an indictment on my sisters, who are amazing, hardworking, fiercely resilient human beings who sometimes forget to rest the cape. Amina, Nefertiti, Charlotte, Harriet, Ida, Gertrude, Thelma, Mary, Shirley, Maya, Fannie, Angela, Toni, Serena, Michelle, Kamala — the queens, the firsts, the onlies — these women wore and still wear the cape. We must be at peace knowing there's room for us to take cover and rest under the veil of our sisters should we decide to hang up our cape, even if for a night, a weekend, a month, or a year. We must give ourselves a break.

Dearest Sisters, as we overcome some of the beliefs that do not serve us, remember this:
- No is a complete sentence.
- You do not have to be all things to all people.
- Set boundaries.

- Protect your time.
- You are not a Superhero. Be human.
- Rest.
- Ask for help.
- Find balance in all things.
- Be intentional about the person you wish to become.
- Embrace all that you are and all that you are not. You are enough.
- If you are constantly the smartest person in the room, get out and go to a different room.
- You can be replaced at work. You cannot be replaced at home. Make home a priority.
- Forgive those who think you are committing an act of tyranny because you are making time for yourself.
- We all want what's best for our kids. You are a good mom. Be okay with that. Doing the most isn't necessary.
- And by any means necessary, love yourself.

Shonda and I journeyed through coming to terms with what we want for ourselves and who should be the most important people in our lives. She didn't know she was worthy of saying yes, and I didn't think I was worthy of saying no. Now I do.

Sissac is a proven communications strategist with over 30 years of experience working for global professional services companies, public relations, and advertising firms, nonprofits, and regional philanthropic organizations, while building consensus and engagement with diverse networks.

Sissac currently leads marketing and communication initiatives in St. Louis, Missouri, and Minneapolis, Minnesota, for Accenture, a leading global professional services company offering consulting and strategy in technology and security. She previously served as Deputy Director for the Regional Arts Commission of St. Louis.

A native St. Louisan and respected civic volunteer, Sissac's community involvement spans over 25 years, focusing on the well-being of children and fostering economic development for under-resourced communities. She currently co-chairs the Diversity, Equity, Inclusion, and Accessibility Committee and the Audience Development Committee of the Saint Louis Symphony's Board of Trustees.

Sissac is a writer, poet, and public speaker who focuses on children's advocacy issues and economic advancement for black women and marginalized communities.

www.linkedin.com/in/sherry-sissac/

www.facebook.com/sherry.sissac

www.sherrysissac.com

Simone M. Cummings

Your Path is What You Make It

Two roads diverged in a yellow wood,
And sorry I could not travel both...
Two roads diverged in a wood, and I –
I took the one less traveled by,
And that has made all the difference.

– Robert Frost

We all encounter forks in the road — do we go left, or do we go right? There is no simple road map or GPS locator telling us the appropriate path. There is often no "right" or "wrong" choice. In this chapter, I'll share with you lessons I've learned about overcoming bumps in the road as I navigate my path forward.

Axiom #1: Planning is Everything!

A good friend once told me it seems as though everything always works out for me. And in fact, it has been my experience that this is mostly true. As I spoke with another friend about this idea, he noted that the obstacles I face are no different from those experienced by others. What is different, he suggested, is how I approach them.

I believe strongly in the benefit of being prepared. I tell my students that to get the job they ultimately want, they need a plan for achieving their goals. More specifically, I never fail to talk about the benefits of having Plan A, Plan B, and even Plan C. You never know when you'll experience a roadblock in life, but when you anticipate problems, you're always prepared.

Years ago, I worked in administration for a hospital that began having financial difficulty. I thought about going to graduate school but hadn't yet applied. Given the hospital's financial situation, I decided to move up my timetable. Several months later, I was asked to eliminate a position from the department I managed. I recommended that my position be eliminated and that my department be combined with another, and this is what happened. Rather than being a challenge for me, the situation ended up being an opportunity. I had already been accepted into graduate school and was able to take the entire summer to relax before the start of school. However, I wouldn't have been prepared for a layoff if I had not planned for this contingency. The situation would have seemed more of a roadblock than the opportunity I ultimately experienced.

Axiom #2: You Control Your Happiness!

When I was in college, I read a book for one of my courses that significantly impacted my thinking about how I experience my personal feelings. The book's author suggested that individuals can choose how they feel, which was novel thinking to me. Up to that point in my life, I believed that external factors caused me to be happy, angry, or sad. For example, if something good happened to me, I'd feel happy. If something bad happened, I'd feel angry or sad.

The idea that I could choose my feelings resonated with me, especially because I liked the idea of having more control over my mental state. I decided I could and should choose to be happy as much as possible. And it worked. Instead of worrying over specific issues, I began taking time to analyze them and focus on what could happen should the worst possible course of action occur. In every situation, I understood that my blessings always outweighed any negative outcomes. Even in the midst of the possibility of the worst outcome, I knew I'd still have support from my family.

My father, with whom I was very close, passed away last year. And while I was sad, it was always my dad's belief that once someone is gone, they're gone and in a better place. Rather than focusing on my loss, I decided to focus on that sentiment, knowing this is what he believed. I decided how I wanted to feel and chose how I experienced his loss.

Daily, I choose happiness, and it influences my personal and professional relationships. When people speak about me, they often note that I always have a smile on my face and a positive attitude. Positivity breeds positivity. What I send out into the world comes back to me many times over. And as a result, good things tend to happen for me. Choosing happiness will provide you with benefits for a lifetime and turn any obstacles you face from mountains into molehills.

Axiom #3: The Past Is in the Past!

A friend told me recently that she was passed over for a promotion because her supervisor and colleagues "didn't like" her. I tried to provide her with several options for moving forward, but she noted that none would ever work because it didn't change the facts as she saw them. My friend will never move forward until she stops focusing on the past.

Disappointing things happen to us all, but we need to take those disappointments and figure out how to leverage them into opportunities. When I was younger, I applied for a hospital evening administrator position for which I was eminently qualified. The chief executive officer (CEO) had been one of my professors and thought very highly of me and my work ethic. During my interview, the CEO told me that although I was very qualified, the hospital wasn't ready for someone like me — meaning the hospital wasn't ready to have an African American woman serve as the evening administrator.

As disappointing as this situation was, it didn't keep me from moving forward. In fact, I saw this as an opportunity to explore other options and ended up obtaining a wonderful internship in another hospital system. Behind every negative situation is a silver lining — you just need to look for it! Don't let the past keep you from moving forward.

Axiom #4: Be Confident!

I see myself as a confident, strong, and successful African American woman. All that I do in terms of planning, preparation, and attitude, work in concert to help me actualize this vision. Each success I garner further contributes to my belief in myself and my ability to succeed at whatever I undertake.

My level of confidence is visible, and people naturally gravitate toward me. My confidence allows me to think about the possibilities of what might be and supports me in my efforts to take risks because I know that if I attempt to do something and it's unsuccessful, it's not because I wasn't prepared. My belief in myself gives me the freedom to be decisive because I know that I'm making the best decisions possible with the data I have.

From my experience as an academician, the lack of confidence is one of the most difficult challenges some women face. It prevents them from seeing their potential and from achieving their dreams. So, what do you do if you aren't confident or you feel insecure? You fake it until you do.

Dress for the role you want to hold. Smile often. Develop a network of women who can provide you with advice and support. Do your research and be decisive in your decision-making. When you are confident in your abilities, your roadblocks will feel like minor obstacles that are easily overcome.

All of us are on a journey and have many decisions in life to make. No one can travel your path except you. So, plan for your success, be optimistic and forward-thinking. Know that you deserve all the great things that are possible. Believe in yourself, and no roadblocks will prevent you from achieving your goals.

Simone M. Cummings, MHA, PhD, Dean, George Herbert Walker School of Business & Technology, Webster University

Dr. Cummings serves as the chief academic officer for the George Herbert Walker School of Business & Technology. In this role, she's responsible for providing leadership, management, and oversight of all aspects of the Walker School, including program planning and development; enrollment and retention; curriculum; hiring, training, and supervising faculty; accreditation; and business and community engagement — at the primary location in Webster Groves, Missouri, as well as at more than sixty military, metro, and international locations.

Dr. Cummings joined the Walker School in 2013 as an Associate Professor of Management, having previously held faculty positions with Washington University in St. Louis and Simmons College in Boston. She holds a BSBA with a Concentration in Marketing from Washington University, an MHA with a Concentration in Finance from the Washington University School of Medicine, and a Ph.D. in Health Policy and Administration from UNC-Chapel Hill.

Dr. Cummings is a board member of St. Louis Children's Hospital, St. Louis Forum, the St. Louis Regional Health Commission, and the Missouri History Museum Sub-Commission. She's an active tennis player and plays jazz piano. She is married to Don Lawrence, and they have two daughters, Nina and Madison.

www.linkedin.com/in/simone-cummings-66a8224

Desiree Coleman-Fry

The Sound of Magic

Click. Clack. Click. Clack.

When people ask, "What does **Black Girl Magic** sound like?" I say, "It's a beat. It's a rhythm. It's a sway. It's a dance."

It's a beat.

Beat down, mistreated and misused, Fannie Lou Hamer told the world, "We are sick and of being sick and tired."

For example, when the City Council of Greenville, South Carolina, tried to beat the dignity out of Black women and said that whether they wanted to or had to, working in the homes of White women was their duty. Yet, after decades of caring for the needs of others, the Black maternal health crisis threatens our lives, as we try to bring forth life, and the world marches on.

It's a dance that Black women have to play in the workplace, with an identity that traverses race and gender. The dance that requires code switching and tightrope walking. The smooth groove that asks us to face microaggressions and pretend it doesn't faze us. Yeah, it's a dance.

Tressie McMillian Cottom explains, "In a modern society, who is allowed to speak with authority is a political act." So, when Black women speak, with whom we speak, and how we speak are forces that our sisters must constantly grapple with.

It's a beat.

Like the storekeeper that beat the humanity out of Harriet Tubman with an iron that left scars, inside and out. So, she ran until she got free, and she just kept running.

It's a beat…like Jezebel…uh, Sapphire…no Mammy. Forget it — it's all the atrocious stereotypes that dehumanize black women's autonomy and bodies.

It's when Serena Williams refuses to be beaten and insists, "You owe me an apology."

Our resistance endures from the Jamestown slave ships, to the depths of the Bayou, to mob fires in Tulsa, to Chicago's South Side, to a march in Louisville, to Oakland, and the streets of Ferguson, Missouri.

We have rejected the boxes you put us in and dismissed what you told us about our bodies. We've embraced our lips, our hips, and the indisputable truth that 'Black don't crack.'

It's a rhythm, like Willow Smith's, "I whip my hair back and forth," and it's necessary because the Crown Act is not yet national law. And Black women can be discriminated against in many states for how our hair naturally grows out of our head. We're told, "It's unprofessional" at work. Black students are sent home from school for wearing braids and natural styles, proving The Tignon Law that policed Black women's hair in the 18th century is still alive and well.

It's a rhythm, with sultry chords that build us up and remind us that we are young, gifted and Black. Thank you, Nina.

It's a rhythm. Like the vroom of keys to Missy's jeep.

It's a sway, like when the suffragettes refused to sway and fully include Black women, prompting Sojourner Truth's decry, "Ain't I a woman?"

It's a sway, like the noose that hung Sandra Bland and the generational trauma from scores of women who saw their husbands, fathers, brothers, and sons dragged away to be lynched.

It's the sway of our swag that reverberates and invites you to believe in magic. A special kind of magic. Black girl magic.

Black women have always been at the forefront of change, innovation, and resistance. For centuries, Black women have nurtured families and built communities. Our foremothers, like Mary McCleod Bethune, educated us. But, our mamas, aunties, and cousins showed us the formidable love that Black caregivers have for their children. The world has never seen an incomparable "mother-child love" so dear as what emanates from Mother Africa, the mother of all mothers.

Yet, the world has not always been kind to Black women. Bearing the scorn of racism and sexism, we must channel the words of Black women like Maya Angelou to persist and declare, "Still, I rise."

When our bodies are sexualized and weaponized, we channel the words of Toni Morrison who said, "Definitions belong to the definers, not the defined." So, we define ourselves for ourselves, loving every bit of who we are.

When people have the audacity to comment on something so personal as our hair, we continue to shine bright. Whether it's a weave or clean-shaven, twists or Afro puffs, a ponytail or fried, dyed and laid to the side, we embrace the words of India.Arie and affirm, "I am not my hair."

From Cardi to Meg, Black women are the trendsetters in fashion, style, and all that is cool.

Our "je ne sais quoi" is ethereal and intangible, transcending time and space. That's why it's called *Black Girl Magic*.

Black women have been at the forefront of advocating for justice for centuries. When folks think about the suffragettes, many don't think about Black women such as Mary Church Terrell, Ida B. Wells, and Mary Ann Shadd Cary. They wrote, organized and published to ensure women received the right to vote. These women were there in 1913, marching in Washington, DC, during the women's suffrage procession. And when Black women were denied the same rights as White women with the passage of the 19th Amendment, we persisted.

Civil rights activists like Fannie Lou Hamer reminded us that, "Nobody is free until everybody is free." Even with passage of the Voting Rights Act of 1965, the inalienable right to vote remains insecure. So, we lean on the words of Stacey Abrams, who reminds us that, "Our ability to participate in government, to elect our leaders and improve our lives is contingent upon our ability to access the ballot. We know in our heart of hearts that voting is a sacred right — the fount from which all other rights flow."

So, we celebrate women like Miriam Makeba, also known as Mama Afrika, who defied state sanctioned hatred. Her liberation songs became revolutionary and helped to fuel the international movement that tumbled South Africa's apartheid system. And so we rise.

For generations, Black women have been rising above limitations and defying everyone's wildest imagination. Mae Jamison literally defied gravity as she became the first Black female astronaut at the National Aeronautics and Space Administration (NASA). Alice Ball defied conventional wisdom when she leveraged Hawaii's chaulmoogra tree to develop the Ball Method, which became the foundation of treating leprosy in a generation of people.

Shirley Chisholm defied the social order when she dared to believe in herself and become the first black woman to run for president of a major political party. Unbossed and unbothered, she refused to listen to the voices that told her to wait her turn and accept the status quo. When people didn't make room for her, she brought a folding chair to the table.

And when reporters asked Simone Biles why she continued to innovate her sport, soar to new heights, defy expectations and set new records, her answer was surprisingly simple, "Because I can." Because she can, because we can, because Black women can.

When environments ask us to code switch, we remember Sweet Brown and think to ourselves, "Ain't anybody got time for that." In the face of opposition, we muster the grace of Michelle Obama, who told us, "When they go low, we go high."

When society threatens the existence of Black trans women, we remember Audre Lorde, who paved the way for intersectional feminism. As a queer, Black, literary genius she said, "I am not free while any woman is unfree, even when her shackles are very different from my own." This is the truest sense of intersectionality.

Coined by Kimberle Crenshaw, intersectionality highlights the overlapping and compounding impact that individuals with multiple identities on the margins face. These "margins" could be sexual identity, race, gender, ability status, socioeconomic status, and the list goes on. Therefore, appreciating intersectionality is understanding the compounding effects of diverse identities.

Black women are a sisterhood that knows that when one of us wins, we all win. So, we appreciate how Issa Rae roots for everybody Black and how Gwendolyn Brooks reminds us of that sisterhood, saying, "We are each other's harvest; we are each other's business; we are each other's magnitude and bond." Black women are the color of coffee beans and everything in between. From espresso to cocoa. Caramel to a frothy latte, the colors of our hues run the gamut and span the globe. We are a Diaspora. Beyoncé gave us our freedom song *cry, Brown Skin Girl*, because Black girl magic is a real thing.

It's a beat. It's a rhythm.

It's a sway.

It's a dance.

Click.

Desiree Coleman-Fry helps women live abundantly. She's been featured in Business Insider, Blavity and PBS and was named one of

Hive's 2020 Top Diversity and Inclusion Leaders of North America. With a passion for creating community and connection, Desiree speaks, writes, and curates events to empower women. Inspired by her daughters, she founded the Queen Within (@queenwithinyou), a vibrant, online community focused on women's empowerment. In 2019, the Queen Within's Virtual Women's Empowerment Experience brought together over 1,000 women from across the globe, including 30 states, Canada, the United Kingdom, Malaysia, Australia, and Nigeria to prioritize health, well-being and wellness.

She was selected for LinkedIn's prestigious Creator Accelerator and founded the Women Work Well community, which centers working moms and offers resources to help moms balance work, wellness & womanhood. With a following of nearly 30K on the platform, Desiree uses Women Work Well to show women how to live abundantly, love their babies, and level up in their career.

As a diversity, equity, and inclusion (DEI) executive, Desiree advocates for workplace equity and is the recipient of the 2019 Rising Star in D&I Award from Investment News. She holds a Master of Public Administration from Syracuse University, is a Loyola Academy trustee and resides in St. Louis, MO, with her husband and four children.

www.linkedin.com/in/desireescoleman/
twitter.com/DesireeSColeman
www.facebook.com/desireescoleman
www.instagram.com/desireescoleman/

Janelle Jenkins

Breaking the Mold

When I was younger, I believed that playfulness and glee were best suited for personal time, and focusing on facts and performance, often devoid of feelings, was appropriate for work and school spaces. Even socially, some part of me believed that I had to be smart or fun, but I could not be both. If you met me in a work or school setting, you would not think I loved dancing, laughing, and partying. If you met me at a party, you would not think I was smart. I thought I needed to fit the image of all spaces and keep other people comfortable. I also long believed the adage that I had to work twice as hard as my non-melanated counterparts to get half as far.

My preparation for my first job post-college demonstrates my deeply held beliefs. I graduated from school in late April 2000. I had longed to travel after graduating, but my job began in June, so I sacrificed those post-college celebratory travel plans. My start date was non-negotiable.

I was super excited about my first day of work. For me, a job symbolized adulthood and independence. Weeks before my first day, I chose the perfect first-day "power suit" and heels from my mother's closet (independent adults borrow clothes too). I made a hair appointment for the Saturday before I started. I wanted everything to be perfect. In a summer enrichment program, I learned that you dress for the job that you want, not the one you have. I wanted to ooze professionalism.

On the way to my hair appointment, I learned that my cousin's funeral was scheduled for Monday, my first day of work. My hairstylist accidentally colored my hair fire engine red instead of auburn at the shop. Later that day, I sprained my ankle. I was living Murphy's Law - everything was going wrong. That night, I was bewildered. This was just too much.

While these things were unexpected, I did what I have always done. I hunkered down and made things work. I went to the beauty supply store and purchased brown hair spray to cover my bright hair. I changed my well-planned outfit from a power suit and heels to slacks and flats. I sent my regards to my extended family via my mom, who attended my cousin's funeral. I tightly wrapped my ankle and went to work.

For many years, I considered this day a success. I did not let anything stand in the way of me getting my job done. I added myself to the long line of women who kept performing despite obstacles in their way. I now look at this story as a cautionary tale. I do not live for work. I work to support my way of life.

Now, I expect to be treated well by my friends and employers. I also remind myself to treat myself well. If I am injured and cannot comfortably walk, I should not walk up multiple flights of steps. While getting a tour on my first day, and obviously limping, the manager who greeted me and gave me a tour of the site did not slow his pace or offer the elevator. If I could go back and whisper in my 21-year-old ears, I would tell myself to, at a minimum, request to ride the elevator. There was no prize for walking in pain, as if nothing was wrong. Now, I will only work with organizations that also realize my humanity.

I deeply regret missing my cousin's funeral. If I pass away, my employer will find another person to fill my role. When family members die, their role and their presence are irreplaceable. I now prioritize my family over everything. I should have taken the day off work. If I could go back in time, I would put into perspective how minuscule missing one day of work would be.

I look back and laugh at my hair snafu. That said, some part of me felt that my hair needed to be straight and neutrally colored to be professional. Hair color and style are not indicative of my level of professionalism. Over 20 years later, I now embrace my natural hair pattern; my natural hair is purposely very red in locs. My skills and hair are a package deal.

When I was in my early 20s, I sacrificed parts of myself to fit a mold. To make other people comfortable and happy, I made myself less happy. I look back at my younger self, in her mother's clothes trying to emulate professionalism, and realize that as an executive, I am defining professionalism for those who look to me as a guide. I can shatter the mold.

I am overcoming the need to fit in. My best secret power is my authenticity. As a seasoned executive, I now have more positional power than a freshly minted undergraduate student. As a woman of color, with very afro-centric features: wide nose, dark skin, and nappy hair, housed in a plus-sized body, I will not fit European-centric beauty standards. As a woman, especially a black woman, I will not fit many people's preconceived vision of a leader: slim, tall, athletic, and well-groomed white male. I know, by example, I am helping others broaden their vision of professionalism.

I want to create a professional environment where people feel cared for and valued for authenticity. A respected employee is a healthy, high-performing employee. I ensure that meetings are not scheduled during lunch to provide my team the opportunity to reset physically and mentally. I monitor my team's paid time off and encourage them to use it. When they suggest that they cannot, I remind them that overworking is not an act of heroism.

I share my expectation that good employees are happy, healthy, and whole. I hold myself responsible for creating a culture that asks people if they need an elevator when limping, demonstrates that hairstyle and color do not impact their work quality, and clearly and openly invites all staff to prioritize their families' needs through equity-focused company policies.

Every day, I am overcoming the need to fit a mold while working on modeling authenticity.

Janelle Jenkins currently serves as the Chief Operating Officer for NCJW – National Council of Jewish Women.

She is a strategic visionary leader with more than 20 years of experience building and optimizing systems, developing leaders, and empowering staff in public and private sectors of banking, manufacturing, and education. She uses her talents to improve her community with a specific focus on bettering the lives of people of color, women, and children.

Born and raised in Detroit, Janelle earned her BBA from Ross School of Business at the University of Michigan, MBA from Booth School of Business at the University of Chicago, and M.Ed in Educational Leadership from The Broad Center. Janelle currently serves as the President of Operations for KIPP St. Louis Public Schools.

As a proud aunt of six and never-nester, Janelle finds joy in writing poetry and short stories, traveling, and dancing everywhere like the world is her living room.

www.linkedin.com/in/janellerjenkins

Kimberly Stemley

Are Giants Five Feet Tall?

As I watched a documentary on the life of the iconic artist and musician Janet Jackson, I realized she and I have something in common. I was glued to the TV for this 4-part special because a part of me was reliving my childhood. Her songs were the soundtrack to my childhood and young adult life. My friends and I would take hours recreating and performing the videos and dance routines in the living room. There were moments I swear I should have had a black cap, a hoop earring with a key attached, and been dancing to Rhythm Nation on MTV. Then there was that smile, her unforgettable sweet, heartwarming smile. Yet, as I kept peering at the screen, there was something familiar about her story and her life. I saw her cute little face as the baby in the famous Jackson family evolve into a young beautiful, woman, singer, actor, dancer, movie star, and legend. So far, this part doesn't look very much like me at all. But taking a closer look, I see 2300 Jackson Street, the small two-bedroom house in Gary, IN, where Janet Jackson's humble story begins. Over the next five decades, she would spend her life touring the world, selling millions of albums, and being recognized as a household name. This wasn't the image she had of herself at 2300 Jackson Street, and for a very long time, she struggled to overcome an identity of small beginnings.

This juncture is where I see myself in the life of Janet Jackson. She didn't come here knowing she was great even though greatness was all around her and literally in her DNA. My life plays to a similar tune. I grew up in Florissant, MO, in Territory Square Apartments with two bedrooms, one designated for my mom and the other for my grandmother and me. I realized I never had a room to myself until becoming a teenager in the 9th grade. Until then, it was "Mother," as we affectionately called my grandmother, and myself sharing a room and bed, might I add. The apartment was small, but we always had what we needed.

I was raised by a single mother, and a grandmother who used a wheelchair due to a crippling work injury. I never identified with being poor but always had a strong identity of being different. The "d" word, different, is kryptonite to any kid. A single black mother, having a child at 43 and serving as the primary caregiver of an elderly disabled woman was not an easy feat. Much later in life, I understood the emotional and mental strain on my mother. Many of my friends came from two-parent homes and had all the amenities that a two-person household could bring. The living experiences of many of my friends and classmates were different from mine. Somewhere along the way, I equated this difference to mean better than. In other words, they were better than me. This very small belief early on in life would prove to be a defining obstacle to achieving greatness.

Overcoming starts with overcoming the small image we have of ourselves.

I also need to interject, I am 5 foot 2 and a buck and a quarter pounds. I have spent my life being physically smaller than most classmates, colleagues, and the world in general. This stature always created a youthfulness that made me appear to be the youngest person in most rooms, and most of the time, I was. Initially, this didn't bother me because I always felt big. I would even get shocked if I got a glimpse of myself and another colleague in the mirror because they looked like a giant over me, although I was the one that felt like the giant. This image always felt a little deflating, but I got over that. It was the attempts of my colleagues and superiors to muffle my voice or outright steal it that were heartbreaking. The first time my superior stole my idea, I was so foolish that I got impressed. I remember thinking, "Wow, they actually used my idea. That's pretty cool!" Slowly, I realized that my ideas for company growth and branding strategy discussions were landing in presentations and board rooms, all without me at the table. It felt like I was told to sit at the kiddie table, yet my ideas were being briefed at the adult table. How could this happen to the same person that felt like a giant? Because somewhere inside me, I agreed with their small image. I still saw myself as the little girl from Territory Square Apartments, sleeping in the bed with grandma.

How could this "little girl" have million-dollar ideas and lead million-dollar initiatives? So, I was baited for concepts and logistics, only for them to resurface as someone else's ingenuity! It was extremely hurtful, degrading, and damaging. After years of mistreatment — I got tired of it and demanded that my voice be respected. In the world of business, the only thing that talks is money! So, I kept talking, freely shared my initiatives and strategies, but this time it came with a price tag — a promotion, a higher salary, and a seat at the table. Although a painful process, my eyes were finally opened to a threat that had been trailing me all along — the little version of myself.

Overcoming deals with trusting yourself in tough times and difficult spaces.

I learned that I possessed strength and the power of creativity, but when my very identity is threatened, I still run back to Territory Square Apartments. Only this time, I returned with an expanded truth of the little girl sleeping in her grandmother's bed — the truth of being raised by two powerful black women. One, defying the odds of an uneducated southern woman, discarded by society and disrespected by judicial systems. My grandmother taught me dignity and strength. She was unapologetically strong in a small crippled vessel. Every night until 9th grade, I was given the privilege of sleeping in the same bed with a little vessel of power. My mother, raised by an uneducated woman, was the first in our family to graduate from college and to experience a successful 32-year career in the U.S. Department of the Army as a high-ranking GS-13. She was a silent giant, defying odds in a white male-dominated environment. Together, these two women raised a 5'2" fusion of dynamite, marching into board rooms and gracefully impacting the world. They raised a CFO of a $60 million pharmaceutical company and regionally recognized nonprofit leader, a speaker at the United States Senate on Aging requesting and helping raise $500 million for Alzheimer's research, and a worldwide philanthropist and humanitarian in the Territory Square Apartments.

There is no overcoming without truly knowing yourself. Why are you a good leader? Why do people listen to you? What is the biggest asset you bring to the team? What keeps you motivated? What makes you a star player? Within the answer to these questions lies your strength to conquer painful and hard times. The first place that a challenging moment in life will attack is your self-identity. The thoughts of can you get through this? Are you really that good? Who said you were capable of this? These thoughts will flood your mind when challenges and new opportunities present themselves. Immediately these thoughts will try to limit your reach by limiting your image of yourself. Adopting a small view of yourself is catastrophic and will stifle your true ability to overcome giant-size problems. It is oppressive in nature to keep any form of life in a vessel that's too small. Even the Humane Society would be called for mistreating animals if we kept a St. Bernard in a cage built for a Chihuahua. Then what is the measure of cruelty for dwarfing your dreams and capacity for greatness? What small images do you have of yourself? What is a constant threat and attack on your very identity as a leader? Everything that comes to attack your identity, dreams, and future is an oppressor, and the first thing an oppressor does is make you feel low, inferior, or flawed in some way. This is a common and usually effective attack that destroys people's mobility and future because they believe in the small image of themselves.

The word "overcoming" implies a fight! The biggest part of this battle is always internal, therefore, establishing a firm identity of self, building a memoir of past successes and strengths, and constantly grasping for the bigger version of yourself will keep you in a constant state of overcoming.

To keep from being prey, I have an ever-evolving view of myself. Life will continually provide threats, curveballs, and obstacles, so I build myself up internally to shut them down every time. Whether you see yourself ascending to the helm of a Fortune 500 company or you're too scared to speak up in meetings, I can guarantee you — you're bigger than you think!

Kimberly has more than 18 years of experience in Finance, Business Strategy, and Development; with positions in public accounting at Ernst and Young, AT&T telecommunications company, and Innovator, an engineering firm previously recognized in St. Louis' Top 50 Fastest-Growing Companies.

She has served as a leader in healthcare as the Executive Vice President, Business Development, and Chief Financial Officer at Rx Outreach, the nation's largest nonprofit, mail order pharmacy, and Patient Assistance Program. To date, she is the Chief Financial Officer of the YWCA Metro St. Louis, recognized by the St. Louis Business Journal as one of the largest nonprofits in the region.

Kimberly's voice is in demand, with requests from board rooms to the White House. Her daily focus has been simple — ensuring the most disenfranchised in our region and the world have access to a better life.

www.linkedin.com/in/kimberly-stemley-96b82238/

Lisa Michelle Garnett

Don't Let Your Dreams Turn Into Nightmares

Bounce back: "to quickly return to normal condition after a difficult situation or event." (Merriam-Webster Dictionary, 2012)

Growing up in the murder capital of the country in the 70s and 80s, watching friends and family succumb to poverty, drugs, alcohol, and, all of the other conundrums of life would leave anyone with a story to tell; here's mine:

I grew up in a single-family home in a dilapidated, not-exactly-thriving community on the north side of the city of St. Louis, Missouri. My brother, Kevin, and I spent most of our time being carted around from our own home church services to other churches where my mother, grandmother, and great-grandfather would bring people to The Father. We spent many nights sweating through our church clothes while cracking jokes in the back pews of sanctuaries whose walls could tell our secrets.

When she wasn't serving the church wearing one of her many hats, my mother spent her days providing for my brother and me and ensured that we never lacked anything. Home-cooked meals, friends, family, and genuine love abounded in my childhood. My brother and I lived in the house with my mother, grandmother, aunt, and cousins, whenever they'd float in. Somehow, there was always just enough space for everyone to be comfortable. There really is something incredible about having a family who consistently prays together.

I excelled in school, and thanks to my mother's unrelenting desire to give us the best, I was able to go to private school up through high school. I excelled wonderfully in music, math, and science, and I graduated as valedictorian of my high school class. I was disciplined, I learned, and I performed well academically, however, it was never my desire to go to college. I didn't see the value of it at the time. MY dream was to be a hairstylist.

I went to school for Pharmacy, with a scholarship to a prestigious university in St. Louis, where most of my tuition expenses were paid. I went to college, falling under the pressure of my family to make something of myself. Living out others' expectations for me, I quickly discovered what I already knew to be true, that while I could excel academically, this simply was not my passion.

Shortly after starting college, I found out I was pregnant with my first child. I was 19-years old, in school where I had no desire to be, working dead-end jobs to put a little money in my pocket. Now, I had to wear this shame publicly in front of all of the church folks who already judged me. After giving birth to my beautiful baby girl, I attempted to go back to school the following year, but things weren't working out for me. I struggled harder than I expected to, juggling motherhood and what I wanted for my life. Eventually, I left school and worked a few odd-end jobs.

Somehow, I landed in cosmetology school in 1991, when my daughter was two-years-old. I was exhausted with the humdrum of my life and needed something that I could stick to and feel fulfilled. Time was of the essence, so I completed my courses for my manicuring license for nails in just three short months instead of securing my cosmetology license, which had always been my dream. After working in a few salons for a few years, I found myself working as a pharm tech in Walgreens, where I met my first husband. We married and had a daughter together.

Our daughter was premature, born at 23 weeks. The doctors told us that our one-pound, six-ounce baby would not live overnight, let alone 24 hours. Furthermore, if she made it past the 24-hour mark, there would be irreparable damage to her bodily functions. She'd use a wheelchair and would never live an independent life of her own. After five months in the NICU, we finally brought our miracle baby home. She grew healthy and strong and eventually went off to school and lived the exact opposite of how the doctors said she would. To God be the glory!

Between caring for our daughter, fulfilling our obligations as parents to our other children, handling ministry obligations, our marriage became secondary to life. We divorced while our daughter was young, amicably parting ways. I kept living my life with my two children, and we thrived and lived happily. I participated heavily in church and found myself mimicking my mother, dragging my children on my hip from one service to another. My children still tell stories about how much time we spent at church, joking that we essentially lived there.

While working in ministry, taking care of my children, and tending to my aging mother and grandmother, I reconnected with the man who would be my second husband. He and I had known each other for several years, and things just never worked out. We were certain that this time things would be just fine. We dated for a while, and it didn't take us long to decide that we wanted to be married. Shortly after that, I gave birth to my final child and my only boy. Our family was complete with two big sisters, and all was well.

When our son turned a year old, my husband was forced to tell me something that would destroy our marriage and affect every relationship I had from that point on. He said he had slept with another woman and that this woman was pregnant. I was devastated. He was my soulmate. Not only had my husband had sex with and impregnated another woman, but my entire inner circle knew.

Hurt, embarrassed, and unsure of where to turn, the only logical option seemed to run away from the situation. Breaking myself away from the things that hurt me made sense, right? We packed up and moved to Detroit, Michigan, in 2005. Things weren't easy, by any means. We lived as happily as we could, and we had some great times. I was still struggling, but for the sake of my children and my marriage, I tried to make things work. A year later, our great times ended, and my husband and I divorced. We split, and I moved back to my hometown. He stayed in Michigan.

Still holding my manicuring license, I made money in salons, building my clientele and making true friends with my coworkers. It was really still my desire to own my own nail shop. I prayed and labored for this shop. In 2006, I opened my own nail studio. Finally, I figured it out. I'd gotten to a place where I worked for myself, I made enough to support my children and myself, and I could be comfortable enough to travel and enjoy the luxurious things in life. I regained my mental clarity in this shop, heard from God, and understood my purpose. I was called to serve.

I'd been in the nail business for about 20 years, however, running a business wasn't always easy. Working for yourself means lots of sleepless nights trying to figure out where to put money for all of your bills. Being a parent also meant missing out on opportunities because my children had things to do. Somehow, while working 12-hour days frequently, I still made the time to take my children to and from school. I never missed a dance recital, math competition, basketball game, or talent show for my children, and for that, the hard work has been so incredibly worth it.

In 2007, I accepted my call into ministry and began becoming a licensed minister. I continued to work and take care of my children. My oldest daughter started college that year, my middle child was in the fourth grade, and my baby boy was four years old. They were settling into their own lives, and so was I. Things were going so well for us, and I was on my way to being happy.

Shortly after this, my grandmother passed away. It shocked all of us. Her legacy touched every family member and permeated our church, and now she was gone. My mother took it very hard, as did my children, especially my oldest. I buried myself into my ministry work and my business to cope with the pain of divorce and the heartbreak of grief.

In 2013, a shift happened, and I closed my shop. At the urging of my pastor, I began working for the church full-time. I excelled at being the executive administrator for my church, and I enjoyed it. At the urging of my pastor yet again, I went to school for computer technology. School was grueling in a way that I didn't expect, but in 2017, I graduated summa cum laude from Ranken Technical College. Not long afterward, I landed a job with a multi-million-dollar company, and I enjoyed the work at first. The stress wasn't worth the pay, and I quit.

I went back to working for my church full-time, and it was just as fulfilling as before. My Bishop connected me with a woman whose passion was to do business with the underserved. She became a vital part of our ministry, and eventually, she needed a Director of Operations at her small business. I decided to take the opportunity! An incredible experience, I am so grateful for the time I've spent there. However, I believe that God is calling me to something greater. I am making enough money, excelling, and being challenged in a way that I enjoy.

After all that I have experienced and every challenge that I have overcome, I now understand that this life I'm living has to truly be my own. No more living up to others' expectations. I can make my own decisions and create a life I truly desire to live. Otherwise, what is the point? The power that I possess can turn nightmares back into the beautiful dreams they were supposed to be. God truly gives beauty for ashes.

Lisa M. Garnett is a native of Saint Louis, MO, and is the oldest of two children. She was the proud owner of The Ben Jacobs Nail Salon in University City, MO.

In 2015 she went back to school, and in 2017 graduated Summa Cum Laude from Ranken Technical College, with a Certification in Computer Networking and Technology.

Lisa currently works as the Director of Operations at Pathways United, and is Campus Pastor of the Cathedral at Pleasant Grove Church, St. Louis, MO, under the leadership of Bishop Courtney Allan Jones. Her great-grandfather started this ministry, and she is honored to continue his legacy.

As a woman of strength and courage who possesses a sincere passion for serving others and spreading God's love, she is the mother of three wonderful children. Lisa is no stranger to struggle or emotional and physical challenges. Yet, she understands that with God on her side, she is more than a conqueror and an overcomer!

www.facebook.com/lisa.garnett.12

www.instagram.com/iamlisagarnett/

Dr. Maurya Dominica Cockrell

Becoming the Grief Walker

 I no longer view grief as an enemy, but I will never consider him a friend. Grief is a visitor that sometimes comes by unexpectedly or gives months' notice; however, I am never prepared for the stay. Over the years, I learned I could overcome the death of a loved one, but I will walk with grief every day.

 My life story is shaped by the who, what, when, how, and I learn more about the why every day. I grew up a happy child, blessed with a two-parent household and grandparents who spoiled me rotten. I never lacked love and enjoyed the closeness of my family. School day mornings were spent with my maternal grandparents, Friday nights were reserved for family catfish dinners, and Sundays were devoted to big family soul food dinners after church.

 My first visit from grief was in 1999 with the loss of my Aunt Virdomae. Since I was only seven years old, I did not fully understand the what, how, and why, but I could feel the loss of "the who." My aunt and I shared a special bond; after all, I was given her middle name, Dominica, and it was at her house where I took my first steps. I watched as grief overstayed his welcome during her many months of illness and hospice care. I wondered why he had come to visit in the first place. One thing for sure, from our first meeting, I knew I never wanted him to visit again. Little did I know he would make me the woman I am today.

From 1999 to 2003, I learned how to function despite the loss. Our schools and workplaces put a time limit on grief. American society tells us to hurry and get over grief or avoid it at all costs. During these years, I learned how to function despite the heartache. I remembered the lessons Aunt Virdomae taught me from elementary to middle school. We expect children to be strong and do not always make space for them to express their grief. Not understanding does not necessarily mean that pain is not felt. Grief decided to visit not once but twice in 2004. I lost my first grandparent, Grandmother Katie, and a few months later, I lost my PaPa. At the age of twelve, I better understood the what and the how. I learned that grief traveled with his suitcase filled with diabetes and Alzheimer's. Once again, I learned how to publicly grieve for the typical three to five days it was acceptable to miss school. Although grief was still in town, I was expected to return to school and focus on academics.

Though I gained resilience along the way, and even though grief called ahead, my metaphorical house was not quite ready for his visit in 2008. February 2008, I lost my grandfather to cancer. In that same month, I learned my MeMe, my grandmother and best friend, was diagnosed with breast cancer at age 83. Little did I know, grief had made plans for an extended stay. I had no extra space for my new roommate, but he made sure to bring a suitcase full of loss, sorrow, and unexpected tragedy. For two years, anticipatory grief would follow me to class, school dances, and even my high school graduation. After MeMe passed in 2010, I thought grief would finally leave so that I could start my life. I decided to stay in

St. Louis and attend Saint Louis University to study health management. Sometimes, I would forget grief was there as I began to enjoy the experience of being a college student, living on campus, learning adulthood.

At this point, I thought I understood grief pretty well. I was familiar that he could be anticipatory, complicated, cumulative, and chronic, but grief had saved something for 2011. On a Sunday afternoon, spring semester, I met grief's traumatic side. I lost my last living grandparent, my grandma Gladys, in a fatal robbery.

Strength and resilience were replaced with anger and fear. Grief left me with the souvenirs of anxiety and depression, but also with a gift that said: "open at a later date." The gift turned out to be faith. After years of viewing grief as my enemy, I began to understand there must be a why. Those losses influenced me to study theology as a minor and directed me towards a path in health, human resources, and spirituality.

Grief moved out from 2012 to 2019, but would always call, email, or text from time to time. These check-ins would come in the form of memories, sadness, and tears, but I learned to use those experiences to help me help others. In 2017, I founded Leaves Speak Healthcare, an intergenerational healthcare consulting company that offers interpersonal skills training for caregivers, community-wide health promotion, death/elder doula services, and healthcare experience designing. I used my personal experiences to work with individuals, families, and communities to walk with grief and focus on legacy. Professionally, I have found roles that allow me to help others during life's challenging times. I have assisted individuals with terminal illnesses to redefine the meaning of work/life balance. I have worked with healthcare providers who struggle to accept the loss of their patients. I have also worked with residents in long-term care facilities actively fighting grief.

While helping individuals navigate grief and loss in the workplace, assisting clients through losing loved ones due to the pandemic, and guiding the community through collective grief from losing beloved celebrities, grief personally came to visit me again in 2020 with the loss of my Uncle George. Unexpected and, of course, unwelcomed, I let grief in to visit. Grief returned to the space I had cleared for him in 2011. I learned the hard way to leave room because I knew grief would always return. Grief's gift of faith had prepared me for this visit. Equipped with faith, I served as a death doula for my family, providing emotional support during our time of loss. Grief left for a short while, then came to visit again later that year with the loss of my Uncle Earnest, and once more in March 2021 with the death of my Uncle Eugene.

These losses finally led me to the why. For me, grief was necessary. In all the pain, planned and unexpected, I found my purpose. My "why" is to help the vulnerable and the bereaved. My professional training in spiritual care and experience as a death doula, paired with my circumstances, led me to my career path. I now work on end-of-life planning and legacy building at individual, institutional, and community levels.

I learned that work and life cannot always be separated. A loss will come that will undoubtedly disrupt how you show up to work, interact with family, and connect with friends. Our emotional well-being touches every area of how we work, live, learn, play, and pray.

To Aunt Virdomae, Grandmother Katie, PaPa, Grandpa, MeMe, Grandma, Uncle George, Uncle Earnest, and Uncle Eugene, you will forever be part of me. I will continue to speak your names so that you are always remembered.

To grief, you will always be an unwelcome guest, but I have overcome the fear of your visits because they have made me the Grief Walker."

Dr. Maurya Dominica Cockrell is an international author, international speaker, and practitioner from St. Louis, MO. Known as the SDoH [social determinants of health] Solutionary, she uses health, education, and human resources to improve how people live, learn, work, pray, and play. In 2015, she began her entrepreneurial journey as an organizational development consultant. In 2017, she founded Leaves Speak Healthcare, an intergenerational healthcare consulting company that offers clients powerful new ways to eliminate ageist "elderspeak" (condescension aimed at older adults), increase compassionate communication, and improve end-of-life acceptance.

Maurya holds a BS in health management from Saint Louis University, with a minor in theological studies, an MA from Webster University in human resources management, and a doctorate in health professions education from Logan University.

She has received additional training and certifications, including Senior Professional in Human Resources (SPHR), SHRM Senior Certified Professional (SHRM-SCP), Evidence-Based Design (EDAC), Death Doula, Spiritual Care Generalist, and Happiness Coach.

md@drmauryadominica.com
www.linkedin.com/in/mauryadc/